# DATE DUE

|  |  |  |  |
|---|---|---|---|
|  |  |  |  |
|  |  |  |  |
|  |  |  |  |
|  |  |  |  |
|  |  |  |  |
|  |  |  |  |
|  |  |  |  |
|  |  |  |  |
|  |  |  |  |
|  |  |  |  |
|  |  |  |  |
|  |  |  |  |
|  |  |  |  |
|  |  |  |  |
|  |  |  |  |
|  |  |  |  |
|  |  |  |  |

Demco, Inc. 38-293

New Dire

**Eliminating A**

D0029647

# New Directions in Special Education

## Eliminating Ableism in Policy and Practice

**THOMAS HEHIR**

HARVARD EDUCATION PRESS
CAMBRIDGE, MASSACHUSETTS

Riverside Community College
JUL '07 Library
4800 Magnolia Avenue
Riverside, CA 92506

LC 3981 .H44 2005

Hehir, Thomas.

New directions in special
   education

Second Printing, 2006

Copyright © 2005 by the President and Fellows of Harvard College

All rights reserved. No part of this publication may be reproduced or
transmitted in any form or by any means, electronic or mechanical,
including photocopy, recording, or any information storage and
retrieval systems, without permission in writing from the publisher.

Library of Congress Control Number 2005931447

Paperback ISBN 978-1-891792-61-8
Library Edition ISBN 978-1-891792-62-5

Published by Harvard Education Press,
an imprint of the Harvard Education Publishing Group

Harvard Education Press
8 Story Street
Cambridge, MA 02138

Cover Design: Alyssa Morris

The typefaces used in this book are Castle for display and
ITC Veljovic for text.

*In Memory of Howard Moses*

# Contents

# Acknowledgments

There are many people who deserve thanks for their contributions to this book, too many to mention here. Prominent among them are members of the disability and parent communities who have had a profound influence on me as a special educator. Among these are Judy and Ilsa Heumann, Adrienne Asch, Martha Zeigler, Rich and Amy Robison, Howard Moses, Maryanne Ivy, Marca Bristo, Larry Gorski, and Jim Charlton. I would like to give special thanks to my friends Penny and Joe Ford, who allowed their struggle for disability equity to be highlighted in this book.

I am also grateful to my colleagues at Harvard University who have supported me in both my writing and teaching, including Lauren Katzman, Arun Ramanathan, Alison Gruner Gandhi, Joanne Karger, Wendy Harbour, Rich Reddick, Eddie Mosqueda, Kia Martin, and Dierdre Duckett. I would also like to thank my colleagues in the field who have provided feedback on my work, including Carl Cohn, Judy Elliot, Dave Riley, and Sue Gamm.

Several of my friends have given me strong encouragement while writing this book, including Eric Rofes, Gil Conchas, Dennis Zaia, and Michael Krisa. I also owe a dept of gratitude to my former partner, Chris LeBlanc, who provided great encouragement and feedback during this project.

Finally, I would like to thank my parents, whose love and support provided the foundation upon which my life has been built. Also, my brothers Mike and Dick and the rest of my wonderful extended family provided their support and their love throughout the writing of this book.

# Introduction

I can still recall the smell, a pungent mix of ammonia and human waste. I can still recall the rows of metal beds, the children and adults who were forced to lie in them, day and night. I can still recall the racket in the ward, the bedridden residents' crying, moaning, yelling, and pleading. The year was 1971, and I was an undergraduate taking my first course in special education, called Nature and Needs of the Mentally Retarded. I encountered this scene on a field trip to a state school for the mentally retarded. I kept wondering where the school was.

It was not only the images that stayed in my mind, but also the attitudes expressed by staff. "This is all you can expect of these people. They're severely brain damaged, vegetables." When we returned to the college, we discussed our feelings about what we had seen. Our professor assured us that these children and adults were capable of far more than was apparent during our visit, and that we would visit other sites where we would see that these students could learn and have full lives. These other sites included special schools and classes in which more fortunate students were learning to read, write, and laugh. However, though some children were getting a chance at a better life, children with significant disabilities were not guaranteed a right to an education. They could be denied entrance to school.

My professor predicted that the time would come when all disabled students would be entitled to a public education. He told us about lawsuits and legislative initiatives that were seeking to extend public education to all disabled students. He also showed us a book, *Christmas in Purgatory* by Burton Blatt, a professor of special education at Syracuse University, which exposed the inhumane treatment of people with mental retardation in state schools that was creating a stir in public policy circles. The lesson was clear from my early classes in special education: The conditions evident in the state schools were not the result of mental retardation alone but, rather, the way society responded to mental retardation. That is, society viewed people with disabilities as inherently incapable of learning and responded by institutionalizing them in substandard conditions where they were deprived of the most basic opportunities. Talking to us as special educators in training, our professor made it clear that our job would be to expand educational opportunity to children with mental retardation and to prove society's negative assumptions wrong.

When I finished my undergraduate work, I decided to pursue a master's degree and had the great fortune to study under Burt Blatt. It was a heady time for special education, as lawsuits were proceeding through the courts challenging exclusion from school and exposing the miseries of institutionalization. Syracuse University was in the middle of it all, with Burt serving as an expert witness in several cases. One course I took, taught by Doug Biklen and Bob Bogdan, was entitled Law and Human Abuse. The course focused on how the law at that time was being used to deny people with disabilities basic human rights. These professors argued that this needed to be turned around, that law should promote, not deny, rights. I left Syracuse energized and pleased that I had chosen a career of such importance: teaching students with disabilities.

I returned to Massachusetts and began teaching at a vocational high school, Keefe Tech in Framingham. The school was brand new, and from its inception it included a broad range of students with disabilities. The state had just passed a comprehensive special education law, Chapter 766, which required that all students with disabilities receive publicly funded education in the least restrictive environment. A number of my students at Keefe Tech had started their lives in the state institutions I had visited three years before. Most of the students with disabilities thrived in this new environment, achieving at levels few would have predicted and going on to real, competitive jobs.

Perhaps no group of disabled students has suffered more historically from negative societal attitudes than students with mental retardation. The change in status of this group over the past 30 years demonstrates clearly that attitudes and policy matter a great deal to the real lives of disabled people. The educational status of mentally retarded children and adults, as well as their integration into communities, has improved greatly over the past three decades. The practice of widespread institutionalization that existed prior to the law has been largely relegated to the past. In the early 1970s, the number of children with mental retardation in state institutions was over 100,000, with many living in filth and getting little education (Blatt, 1970; D'Antonio, 2004). By 1990, an approximately 90 percent reduction in institutionalization had occurred (Scheerenberger, 1990). These students are increasingly placed in integrated schools and classrooms. By the 2000–01 school year, fewer than 6 percent of children with mental retardation were educated in separate facilities (U.S. Department of Education, 2003). New approaches have been developed that demonstrate that even students with significant retardation can move from school to supportive, competitive work environments (Mank, 2001). Other innovative educators are demonstrating how even students with significant mental retardation can have access to literacy instruction (Kliewer et al., 2004).

Although there is significant room for improvement, the educational status of these children is in sharp contrast to what it was before the passage of PL 94-142 and Section 504 of the Rehabilitation Act of 1973.[1] Prior to these laws, it was legal to exclude

---

1. Section 504 of the Rehabilitation Act of 1973 was the first federal law that guaranteed education to all disabled children by prohibiting discrimination against the disabled by any institution that received federal funds. Therefore, given the fact that

students with mental retardation from school entirely, and most states did. Some states even required local school districts to exclude students with mental retardation (Hehir & Gamm, 1999). In response to the eugenics movement, policies in the first half of the 20th century had actively sought to separate the "feebleminded" from the rest of society through the development of a vast array of state institutions. Mental retardation was thought to be a hereditarily determined, fixed trait that could be diagnosed based on performance on a standardized intelligence test. These policies created the institutions I visited as a young man. People were literally incarcerated without recognition of fundamental constitutional rights simply by scoring poorly on these tests. The result was that even children without mental retardation, often wards of the state, were placed in these institutions (D'Antonio, 2004).

Blatt's (1970) description of the conditions of "back wards" captures the horrors endured by many people with mental retardation incarcerated in state institutions:

> In each of the dormitories for severely retarded residents, there is what is called, euphemistically, the day room or recreation room. The odor in each of these rooms is overpowering, to the degree that after a visit to a day room I had to send my clothes to the dry cleaners to have the stench removed. The physical facilities often contributed to the visual horror as well as to the odor. . . . Most day rooms have series of bleacher-like benches on which sit denuded residents jammed together without purposeful activity or communication or any kind of interaction. In each room is an attendant or two, whose main function seems to be to "stand around." . . . I was invited into the female as well as male day room, in spite of the supervisor's knowledge that I, a male, would be observing denuded

---

public schools accepted federal money, they were covered under the act. The Individuals with Disabilities Act (IDEA), originally PL 94-142, the Education for All Handicapped Children Act, passed shortly after Section 504 in 1975. PL 94-142 provided funds to states to assist in the education of the disabled, along with significant regulatory requirements. All states eventually chose to accept this money and therefore are subject to the IDEA's regulatory requirements.

females. I noticed feces on wooden ceilings, and on the patients as well as the floors. (p. 16)

Blatt (1970) goes on to describe the abusive conditions encountered by children:

> The children's dormitories depressed me the most. Here, cribs were placed—as in other dormitories—side by side and head to head. Very young children, one and two years of age, were lying in cribs without contact with any adult, without playthings, without apparent stimulation. In one dormitory that had over 100 infants . . . I experienced my deepest sadness. As I entered, I heard the muffled sound emanating from the "blind" side of the doorway calling, "Come, come, play with me. Touch me." I walked to the door. On the other side were 40 or more unkempt infants crawling around a bare floor in a bare room, crying for attention. One of the children had managed to squeeze his hand under the doorway and push his face through the side of the latched door, crying for attention. His moan begged me for some kind of human interaction. (p. 18)

D'Antonio (2004) captures the horrors endured by boys with questionable mental retardation who were placed at the Fernald School in Massachusetts, and their interminable desire for freedom, in *The State Boys Rebellion*. He recounts the actions of one of the more abusive attendants:

> Unlike other violent attendants who were unpredictable and might suddenly become enraged, McGinn was methodical. For example, during almost every meal in the crowded first floor dining room, he walked silently around the tables with a large metal spoon in his hand. A boy who talked too loudly, or at all when McGinn had commanded silence, would get a whack on the head with a spoon. At other times, McGinn declared that he was searching for "hollow heads" and walked his way around the tables thunking as many skulls as he pleased.
>
> Up in the wards, where he was often alone with the boys, McGinn allowed himself to practice sadism with a sexual component. Instead of red cherries, he would have the boys line up, pull down their pants, and stand still while he went down the line yanking on each one's testicles. The pain was almost equaled by

the shame the boys felt as they trembled with fearful anticipation. Many began crying as McGinn approached, well before he even touched them. (p. 45)

In addition to such atrocities, these boys were subjected to medical experiments under the auspices of the U.S. government, Harvard University, and the Massachusetts Institute of Technology, in which they were fed irradiated cereal. Most lived to see the day when President Clinton offered a formal apology to the victims of these experiments (D'Antonio, 2004).

The conditions at Fernald, depicted by Blatt and D'Antonio, were not confined to Massachusetts and were sometimes worse in other states. Geraldo Rivera's historic 1972 exposé of the Willowbrook State School in New York City asserted that 100 percent of the residents contracted hepatitis B within a year of admittance. In 1966, many states were spending less than $6 a day on inmates in state schools for the mentally retarded (Blatt, 1970, p. 186).

The horrors described by Blatt, Rivera, and D'Antonio are largely a thing of the past, due to changes in societal attitudes and the power of more benevolent and progressive public policies reflected in PL 94-142. These changes began when a coalition of parents of children with mental retardation and progressive educators challenged the dominant view of mental retardation as tragic, hopeless, and potentially menacing. This was replaced by an optimistic view that children with mental retardation could benefit from education and supportive families and communities, and that people with mental retardation had rights just like all Americans under the Constitution. They further asserted that institutionalization harmed these children and exacerbated the impact of their disability. Again, Blatt (1970) summed up this view presciently:

Our true mission is to guarantee to every human being the right to be treated as a human being. . . . [O]ur true mission is to eradicate forever the evils of the back wards and the philosophies that breed them, and the conception that those evils resulted from a condition called "mental retardation" rather than a condition called civilization. (p. 253)

We are reinforced again and again in our conviction that intelligence, that all human development, is plastic and a function of practice and training, motivation and stimulation, as well as it is a function of neurology, chromosomes, and genes. (p. 254)

We must develop more optimistic convictions concerning the abilities and potentials of those we call mentally retarded, however severe that mental retardation may be. The prophecy of incompetency and vegetation associated with mental retardation is self-fulfilling. Equally self-fulfilling can be the prophecy of competency and achievement. (p. 258)

Looking back from a vantage point 30 years distant, visionaries like Blatt were clearly correct in their conception of the malleability of mental retardation and wise in their use of rights-based strategies. Their rights-based arguments successfully ended the practice of exclusion, initially through the courts (Hehir & Gamm, 1999) and ultimately with the passage of PL 94-142. The new special education law enshrined rights-based concepts of due process concerning the identification and placement processes of disabled children, significantly curbing the states' power to place children unilaterally in inappropriate placements and giving parents a powerful implementation tool (Hehir, 1990). A new generation of parents has used these tools to promote more inclusive education for their children, continuing a long march toward a brighter future for children with mental retardation (Hehir & Gamm, 1999).

Evidence of a much-improved world for children with mental retardation is everywhere. Most children with mental retardation learn to read. Many play on athletic teams, belong to Scout troops, and participate actively in their houses of worship. Parents write poignant accounts about the gift of their child with mental retardation (Bérubé, 1996). The Special Olympics is a major sports event in its own right. One recent news segment described a new program opening this fall at the University of Southern Maine for young people with developmental disabilities. An incoming freshman with Down's syndrome was interviewed about his future plans, while his mother expressed her long-held desire that her son continue his education after high school. This is a far cry from the institution of the 1970s.

It is important to note that this optimistic picture of the status of education for students with mental retardation is by no means universal. Too many children with mental retardation continue to be inordinately segregated and insufficiently challenged, reflecting continuing low expectations. Some students, particularly racial minorities, continue to be placed inappropriately in special classes (Losen & Orfield, 2002). However, the trends for students with mental retardation are generally positive. Widespread exclusion and institutionalization have been eliminated and major strides toward integration have occurred.

The progress we have made over the last 30 years in the education of children with mental retardation supports the underlying thesis of this book: *Attitudes toward disability have a major impact on the education these children receive.* Changed attitudes toward mental retardation were necessary to challenge the dominant dysfunctional and abusive practices that characterized society's responses to children with this disability for most of the 20th century. Policies and practices have changed radically in a relatively short time. However, it would be a mistake to assume that merely changing attitudes is sufficient. This change was also dependent on the development of new approaches in education and early intervention for these children and their families. Progress has occurred through innovation within a values-based context of optimism propelled by strong law based on constitutional principles of equal rights and procedural due process. I believe that the progress that has occurred for children and adults with mental retardation is the result of the conversion of three forces. First, attitudes toward mental retardation became more benevolent and optimistic. Second, significant changes in care supported more progressive approaches and guaranteed important rights. And third, new approaches and innovations were developed that allowed children with mental retardation to learn at higher levels.

I wrote this book because, as a career special educator, I want both to celebrate the successes of the field over much of the last 30 years and to articulate a future that can build on those successes. However, as one who has a rather unique vantage point due to the various positions I have held, including director of the Office of Special Education Programs (OSEP) for the U.S. Department of Education, I am deeply concerned with the lack of direction of the field. I am further concerned with the fact that large numbers of students with disabilities are not able to benefit from the innovative, research-based practices that have been developed. Thus as we move into a new century in which special education has become a major component of American education, I feel we need to reevaluate the role of special education.

Is our role simply to comply with law or to comply with the spirit of law? Are we simply providers of service, or do we produce results? In an age of standards-based reform and inclusion, what is the proper role for general education, and to what degree are regular educators accountable for students with disabilities? Are the only important results of our efforts performance on standards-based tests, or do we have a more robust agenda? Do we accept dominant negative societal attitudes toward disability, or do we seek to change the world through education?

As I have reflected on these questions, particularly when I became head of OSEP and since that time, I have benefited greatly from the insights of adults with disabilities and of parents of children with disabilities, with whom I have worked and developed friendships. These friends and colleagues brought me to the realization that many of the problems that disabled students experience have discrimination at their core.

I recall a discussion I had with my former boss, then assistant secretary of education and longtime disability activist Judy Heumann, about the exclusion of disabled students from state testing accountability systems. "Why are you surprised Tom? Don't you see it's discrimination? It's ableism. Most disabled people experience that their whole lives because others don't believe they are capable." I was viewing the problem as a policy issue while Judy saw it through a much clearer lens. Though this exclusionary practice is ending due to changes brought about in federal law by disability activists like Judy, discrimination continues. Judy's use of the term "ableism"—deeply held negative attitudes toward disability that are analogous to racism—took me aback. It seemed such a strong word with serious implications. However, as I kept working with Judy and other disability activists, I began to see more clearly how deeply some educational practices reflect this prejudice. Requiring deaf students to lip-read rather than sign, preferring to have children with minimal vision read print rather than learn Braille, expecting dyslexic students to read a textbook far beyond their reading level in order to access a physics class are common examples of practices that I began to see as ableist at their core.

The lens of ableism began to take on great power for me as a special educator and provided a critical way to both evaluate practices and provide direction. It was clear to me that educational practices at times reinforced ableism, while at other times they served as important vehicles to overcome this form of discrimination. However, as I have spoken around the country on this issue, I have become aware of how few of my colleagues have even heard the term.

This book is an attempt to apply the lens of ableism to the field of special education in order to provide direction to a field that seems a bit out of focus. I would love to rekindle among educators and parents the clarity of purpose instilled in me as a young special education teacher, the determination that special education should define itself explicitly as a field that seeks to change negative views of disability while providing students with disabilities access to a quality education.

This book goes beyond the important discussion of attitudes of ableism and how ableism may negatively affect the education of children with disabilities. It focuses also on making the right decisions about the education of children with disabilities: the decisions we make about individual children, the way we provide for their education, and the policies that support progress. It will provide detailed treatment of how we might greatly improve the education of children with disabilities through changing attitudes, innovative practices, and supportive public policy.

The book is organized as follows: Chapter 1 defines ableism in education and gives examples of how these negative attitudes have influenced the education of various groups of disabled students. Chapter 2 addresses the role of special education in promoting educational equity for students with disabilities and proposes a framework on which educational decisions for students with disabilities can be based. Chapter 3 focuses on the issue of placement in general education classrooms or inclusion. This issue has had a major impact on special education and remains controversial among many educators and advocates. Chapter 4 discusses the promise of universal design—the concept originating in architecture that calls for designing buildings, technologies, and services in ways that assume the need to provide access for people with disabilities. This chapter addresses the appropriate design of early reading programs, school discipline and behavior programs, curriculum access, and school structures. Chapter 5 addresses the most pressing policy issues facing students with disabilities today: standards-based reform and high-stakes testing. The chapter concludes with a set of recommendations on how to improve the likelihood that students with disabilities will benefit from these reforms. The book ends with a chapter that recognizes the central role policy has had in expanding educational opportunities for students with disabilities. It includes an in-depth discussion of special education policy.

This book is based on my optimistic view that education holds great promise as a vehicle by which individual children with disabilities can gain access to greater opportunity while at the same time promoting a society that values the equality of all its disabled citizens. In this way, education can continue to change society while opening up educational opportunities to all children.

# 1

# Defining Ableism
# in Education

When Joe Ford was born in 1983, it was clear to the doctors and to Joe's mom, Penny, that he would likely have disabilities. A difficult birth had deprived the baby of oxygen, leaving him brain damaged. What wasn't clear to Penny at the time was that she was entering a new world in which she would have to fight constantly for her child to have the most basic rights, a world in which negative cultural assumptions about disability would influence every aspect of her son's life. She and Joe had entered the world of ableist assumptions.

Penny, who is the mother of eight, remembers an event that made it clear this new world was one of lowered expectations. A visiting social worker from a preschool program for children with disabilities who seemed empathetic and supportive nonetheless made it clear to Penny that she could not have the same dreams and aspirations for Joe that she had for her seven nondisabled children. As Penny explains, "She was aghast that I expected that Joe would one day be employed" (Ford, 1993, p. 102). Later, at a workshop for parents of disabled children, Penny was told that she had to go through a period of mourning the arrival of her disabled child. Deeply insulted, Penny responded, "I have lost a child at birth and I have had a disabled child. I know the difference. My son is a gift, not a tragedy" (p. 101). Like many disability advocates, Penny came to see that while disability is not a tragedy, society's response to it can be.

Former U.S. Assistant Secretary of Education Judy Heumann, now a senior official at the World Bank, put it succinctly: "Disability only becomes a tragedy for me when society fails to provide the things we need to lead our lives: job opportunities or barrier free buildings" (Shapiro, 1994, p. 20). Another activist—an employee of the U.S. Department of Education's Office of Civil Rights (OCR) who had been disabled since childhood—counseled Penny: "Don't assume he has the same educational rights as every other child. You're going to have to fight for that" (Ford, 1993, p. 103). This woman helped Penny understand that federal law—Section 504 of the Rehabilitation Act of 1971—prohibited discrimination against her son and that this law, along with the Individuals with Disabilities Education Act (IDEA), supported Penny's desire that Joe receive a quality education.

Despite these strong laws, existing practices were often difficult to change due to deeply held assumptions about disability. By the time Joe was four, Penny had filed a complaint with OCR against the Chicago Public Schools, seeking Joe's placement in a regular school rather than in the special school into which the school department wanted to place him. She had begun the journey to secure an appropriate education for her son—a journey that led him to Harvard University, where he currently is pursuing his undergraduate degree.

In this chapter, I define the form of discrimination known as ableism and examine its influence on the education of children with disabilities. I show how ableist assumptions undermine the educational attainment of these children, grounding the discussion in the context of the contemporary disability rights movement. This book is based on the relevant research and on the narratives of individuals with disabilities and their parents. I also incorporate my 30 years of experience in the field of education as a special education teacher, local special education administrator, and former director of the Office of Special Education Programs (OSEP) at the U.S. Department of Education (DOE), and my current position as a professor of practice and director of the School Leadership Program at the Harvard Graduate School of Education.

## ABLEISM AND SCHOOLING

The various definitions of ableism in the literature share common origins that are rooted in the discrimination and oppression that many disabled people experience in society (Overboe, 1999; Weeber, 1999). Laura Rauscher and Mary McClintock (1996) define ableism as

> a pervasive system of discrimination and exclusion that oppresses people who have mental, emotional, and physical disabilities. . . . Deeply rooted beliefs about health, productivity, beauty, and the value of human life, perpetuated by the public and private media, combine to create an environment that is often hostile to those whose physical, mental, cognitive, and sensory abilities . . . fall out of the scope of what is currently defined as socially acceptable. (p. 198)

Black disability activist and talk-show host Greg Smith (2001) captures the essence of definitions of ableism in his article "The Brother in the Wheelchair": "I've faced unintentional discrimination, and it's just as damaging as racism. . . . It's called ableism, the devaluation and disregard of people with disabilities" (p. 162).

Applied to schooling and child development, ableist prejudices become particularly apparent. The devaluation of disability results in societal attitudes that uncritically assert that it is better for a child to walk than roll, speak than sign, read print than read Braille, spell independently than use a spell-check, and hang out with nondisabled children rather than only with other disabled students. In short, in the eyes of many educators and society, it is preferable for disabled students to do things the same way as their nondisabled peers.

Certainly, given a world that has not been designed with the disabled in mind, being able to perform in a manner similar to that of nondisabled children gives disabled children distinct advantages. A child who has received the help he needs to walk is at an advantage in a barrier-filled world; a child with a mild hearing loss who has been given the amplification and speech therapy she needs may have little difficulty functioning in a regular classroom.

However, ableist assumptions become dysfunctional when the educational and developmental services provided to disabled children focus inordinately on the characteristics of their disability to the exclusion of all else. Narratives written by disabled people and their parents speak to the deep cultural prejudices against disability that they had to endure from an early age that disability was negative and tragic and that the overriding goal of their young lives must be to "overcome" it (Ferguson & Asch, 1989; Rousso, 1984).

In *No Pity,* his history of the disability civil rights movement, Joseph Shapiro (1994) chronicles the dominant cultural responses to disability. One model is exemplified by the poster children of the muscular dystrophy telethon, whom he refers to as "Tiny Tims" who reinforce "the idea that disabled people are childlike, dependent, and in need of charity and pity" (p. 14). Cyndi Jones, a disability activist and former poster child, argues that "the poster child says it's not okay to be disabled . . . but it says if you just donate money the disabled child will go away" (p. 14). Marilynn Phillips, a professor at Morgan State University who has studied images of these poster children, recalls that the image of the valiant "crippled" child on crutches learning to walk emerged in the mid-1950s. She argues that children like herself who had polio before a vaccine was developed were an affront to the postwar faith in medical technology. Disabled children were portrayed as "damaged goods" who had to try harder to deserve charity and respect (p. 15).

According to Shapiro (1994), the belief that disability could be overcome led to the rise of another dominant image of disability: the inspirational disabled person, or "supercrip." Shapiro argues that this image is deeply moving to many nondisabled people and the press but is widely regarded as oppressive to most disabled people. The extensive press coverage of a blind man who recently climbed Mt. Everest is a good example of the supercrip. Cyndi Jones argues that, like the poster child, this stereotype implies that a disabled person is presumed deserving of pity instead of respect until the person proves capable of overcoming disability through extraordinary feats (Shapiro, 1994). Both of these dominant stereotypes have at their core an ableist perspective: the failure to accept and value disabled people as they are.

Progress toward equity is dependent first and foremost on the acknowledgment that ableism exists in schools. In many schools, disability is not apparently part of the diversity discussion, and disability activists have long recognized the impact of this silence (Rauscher & McClintock, 1996). However, as the country becomes more racially and ethnically diverse, schools are increasingly recognizing the need to include disability as part of their overall diversity efforts. Recently, a local high school student with Down's syndrome whom I had met at a school assembly devoted to issues of disability rights addressed one of my classes. She stated, "There are all kinds of kids at my school: black kids, Puerto Rican kids, gay and lesbian kids. Meagan uses a wheelchair, Matt's deaf, and I have Down's syndrome. It's all diversity." Her high school has done a great job of integrating disabled students and has incorporated discussions about disability into its efforts to address diversity issues: Adults with disabilities address student groups, and disability is presented in a natural way; students learn about people with disabilities who have achieved great things as well as those who live ordinary lives. Furthermore, people with disabilities are not presented in a patronizing or stereotypical manner: Deaf people are not "hearing challenged," nor are people with mental retardation "very special." In other words, ableism is not the norm, and disability is dealt with in a straightforward manner. In schools like this, students with disabilities learn how to be self-advocates (Jorgensen, 1997).

This recognition of disability as a basic diversity issue—that disability is not to be pitied, patronized, or vilified—is important in helping disabled students feel comfortable with their disability. These students are unlikely to progress well in school and in life if they are ashamed of their disability or uncomfortable disclosing it. Without this comfort level students may be incapacitated as they deal with the "difference" issues that arise out of their disability, such as the need for accommodation and support. Therefore, the need to provide a supportive environment in which disabled students can learn is directly tied to improving educational results.

Negative cultural assumptions about disability continue to have a pervasive influence on the education of children with disabilities, contributing to low levels of educational attainment and employment. The assumption that disabilities must be "overcome" means that school time is devoted to various therapies that may take away from the time needed to learn academic material. There is an ingrained prejudice against performing activities in ways that might be more efficient for disabled people but that are different from how nondisabled perform them, such as reading Braille or using sign language. There is considerable evidence emerging that these unquestioned assumptions are handicapping disabled children and are a cause of educational inequities.

In this chapter I illustrate the profound and negative impact ableist assumptions have on the education of children with disabilities, using issues that arise with various groups: the deaf, the blind, students with dyslexia, and students with behavioral and emotional problems.

## THE EDUCATION OF THE DEAF

The education of deaf children provides a compelling example of how ableism has distorted efforts to educate people with disabilities. Unlike some disability populations, such as students with significant cognitive disabilities, educational programs for deaf children have existed in the United States for over 150 years. Therefore, there is significant history and research to draw upon to guide our efforts to improve education for the deaf.

Educators who were deaf themselves heavily influenced some of the earliest educational programs for deaf children. Thomas Gallaudet, an early advocate for educating the deaf, visited Europe in 1816, seeking educational models to bring back to the United States. While in Europe, he met a talented young deaf teacher, Laurent Clerc. Together they opened the American Asylum for the Deaf and Dumb in Hartford, Connecticut, in 1817. The teachers were fluent signers, and most were deaf themselves. By using American Sign Language (ASL), the school demonstrated that literacy could be raised impressively among the deaf (Baynton, 1996). In her landmark study of the impact of a high percentage of deaf people living in a Martha's Vineyard community in the 1800s, Nora Groce (1985) found that graduates of the Hartford School had achieved higher levels of literacy than many of their hearing neighbors. Unlike the deaf, many hearing people had left school early to fish or farm. Some of the less educated hearing people would take documents to their deaf neighbors to have them explained. Deafness was so common on the island that most hearing people learned to sign. As a result of their relatively high level of education, deaf people held many positions of leadership in the community.

Despite these promising early results, the education of deaf children was severely set back by oralism in the latter half of the nineteenth century. Spurred on by the establishment of the Clarke School for the Deaf and by the advocacy of Samuel Gridley Howe, the founder of the Perkins Institute for the Blind, and of educator Horace Mann, the oralist methodology claimed success in educating deaf children by teaching them to lip-read and speak. This method prohibited the use of manual language, as proponents felt that signing decreased the motivation to learn to speak. Another prominent advocate of oralism was Alexander Graham Bell, who was, ironically, married to a deaf woman. He sought to have sign language banned from programs for the deaf. In a speech delivered to the National Academy of Sciences in 1883, Bell further advocated for the enactment of eugenics laws to forbid the "intermarriage of deaf mutes" (Baynton, 1996). As Shapiro (1994) points out:

> Oralism fit well with the conformist spirit of the times. The Victorian culture was unsparing toward minority culture. . . . If one did not have speech then one did not have language and, went the thinking that dated back to Aristotle, was presumably unable to reason. To remain silent then was to be prey to the devil. All this suggested that deafness was a sickness, something that needed to be cured. Oralism held out the hope of correction. (p. 90)

The influence of Bell and other oralist advocates would prove to be surprisingly enduring, even to this day. For many, the deaf "supercrip" is the deaf person who can read lips and speak, despite the fact that few deaf people master oralism. Under the best of circumstances, only 30 percent of speech can be read from lip movements (Jacobs, 1989; Lane, 1995). Leo Jacobs, a deaf educator, compares lipreading with breaking 80 in golf or painting a masterpiece. Most people who lip-read successfully tend to be postlingually deaf—people who became deaf after they had developed language (Jacobs, 1989).

The grip of oralism on the education of deaf children weakened in the 1960s, when research began to reveal the benefits of manual communication (Stuckless & Birch, 1966). Many educators of the deaf began experimenting with new modes of communication, such as total communication, which involved a combination of speech and signed English. Another method, cued speech, employed hand shapes formed near the mouth to aid lipreading. Though many viewed these innovations as progress, neither of these approaches used ASL the way the Hartford School did a century before. Thus, oralism continued to have a negative impact on the education of deaf children.

In the 1970s, important research in linguistics confirmed what many deaf people already knew: that ASL was a language with its own syntax and grammar and that manual language developed naturally in deaf children similarly to the way oral language developed in hearing children. Timothy Reagan (1985), in his landmark piece in the *Harvard Educational Review,* stated, "ASL's linguistic features are now understood, at least in fairly broad outline. It is a language in every sense of the word, relying on visual, rather than auditory, encoding and decoding. ASL has a complex, rule-governed phonology, syntax, and morphology" (p. 270).

Other research further supports ASL as the foundation for language development and educational attainment for deaf children. A particularly important line of research involves deaf children whose parents are also deaf. These children, about one in nine deaf children, provide an ideal "natural experiment" to test assumptions about language development and to investigate the potential negative impact of ableist assumptions. Most deaf parents communicate with their infants and toddlers in their natural language, ASL. A number of studies have revealed that these children display superior language development and thus obtain higher scores on intelligence measures than deaf children of hearing parents (Courtin, 2000; Sisco & Anderson, 1980; Zwiebel, 1987). Similar findings have been reported in studies conducted on deaf children of deaf families in Denmark, Israel, and Greece (Lane, 1995). Furthermore, it is unlikely that deaf parents carry with them the negative cultural views of people who are deaf. The birth of a deaf baby to deaf parents is not a tragedy to be grieved but rather a celebrated event. I have deaf friends who, upon learning they are about to become parents, have told me that they would prefer that their child be deaf.

Studies of deaf children whose parents are deaf are revealing. These children start school with vocabularies comparable to their hearing peers and have higher levels of educational and occupational success than most deaf children of hearing parents (Lane, 1995). Comparing students entering school with high levels of ASL ability with those who have lower levels, Michael Prinz and Philip Strong (1998) found that those with high ASL ability achieved higher levels of literacy, even when IQ is held constant. The evidence supporting the need to develop manual language in deaf children is so compelling that a National Academy of Sciences study concluded, "Parents and preschool teachers can enhance deaf children's communicative and reading ability growth by beginning early to communicate with these children through finger spelling and manual signing" (Snow, 1998, p. 164).

This research underscores the point that language is the fundamental cornerstone upon which educational achievement is built for all children. Unless children have well-developed language before learning to read, they are unlikely to achieve high levels of literacy (Snow, 1998). Deaf children are no different from their hearing counterparts in this regard. However, the optimal way for these children to learn language is different because they cannot hear.

Though deaf infants and toddlers and their families are entitled to early intervention and special education services from birth, many deaf children of hearing parents start school with vocabularies of fewer than 50 words (Shapiro, 1994). This is likely due to the lack of emphasis on the development of ASL skills in their preschool programs or at home. Further, many of the school programs these children attend do not recognize the importance of developing and using manual language. Though history and recent research converge to provide clear evidence that recognizing the importance of developing manual language in deaf children is the foundation for literacy and for later educational and occupational success, educational practices often do not reflect these findings. In short, many programs still reflect ableist assumptions about the deaf.

It seems clear that deaf children should be encouraged to learn ASL from infancy and that educational programs should recognize that a well-developed ability in ASL is a strength in deaf children on which their future progress rests. The continued adherence to the ableist assumption that it is better for deaf children to lip-read and speak than to learn sign language will surely guarantee poor educational results for this population. A major longitudinal study of postsecondary outcomes for students with disabilities found that only 28 percent of deaf young adults had enrolled in postsecondary academic programs within three years of graduating, compared to approximately 55 percent of youth in the general population (Wagner et al., 1993).[1]

The ultimate institutionalization of ableist assumptions can be seen in a U.S. Supreme Court interpretation of the IDEA in the case of *Rowley v. Board of Education of the Gloversville Enlarged City School* (1993). The Court decided that a deaf girl who was integrated into a regular class was not entitled to a sign language interpreter because she was "receiving benefit"; that is, she was passing. This decision in effect says that it was acceptable for this deaf child to understand only some of what the teacher was saying. Clearly, this girl was not being given the same access to educational opportunity afforded hearing children. Would parents of hearing children tolerate such a standard being applied to their children's education? School board meetings would be full of parents demanding change. However, there are few deaf children, and they are unlikely to sway a school board. In my view, the Court failed to serve its role of protecting the minority interests of a deaf student from the rule of the majority, the school board.

Though the deaf community may have lost in *Rowley*, it has been using its political power to advocate for significant changes in educational programs for deaf children. Deaf children's low lev-

---

1. I have chosen not to address the issue of cochlear implants in this article due to the complexity of the issue and the relative newness and rapidly changing nature of these devices. Though there is much controversy surrounding these devices, there is evidence that they can increase language development in deaf children. However, more research is needed to determine whether these devices can, by themselves, substitute for the development of language that can occur when deaf children are given access to American Sign Language (ASL) from birth. For this reason, some cochlear implant advocates recommend that ASL be taught to these children as well (Zwiebel, 1987).

el of educational attainment has been the rallying point, and federal intervention has been sought. It is noteworthy that although there has been a significant deaf intellectual community in the United States since the founding of Gallaudet University in 1864, deaf people have not had a significant influence on policy making involving their own education. This was brought into sharp relief during the naming of a new president for Gallaudet in 1988. When two deaf applicants were passed over for a hearing candidate, the campus erupted in protest and the university was closed down (Shapiro, 1994). The deaf student body refused to accept the continuation of the school's 124-year history of having a hearing president at the premier institution for the deaf. After a well-organized protest that included appeals to the U.S. Congress and the president of the United States, a deaf individual, I. King Jordan, was named president.

Another example of the increased role of deaf adults in policy making occurred in 1990 with the issuance of the Deaf Education Policy Guidance by the deaf assistant secretary of education, Robert Davilla. This document emphasizes the importance of language development and communication in the education of deaf children. When Judy Heumann became assistant secretary in 1993, she and I reissued the guidance at the urging of the deaf community. When the IDEA was reauthorized in 1997, the deaf community sought and achieved some significant changes to the IDEA that further supported the centrality of language development and communication in the education of deaf children.[2] Since 1997, the IDEA has required that when an individualized education program (IEP) is developed for a deaf child, the child's

2. At the time of this writing the IDEA has been reauthorized by Congress and signed by President Bush. However, the regulations had not been completed. Thus, "IDEA 2004" used henceforth refers to the current statute and not the regulations. When I refer to the current regulations, I mean the 1997 regulations that continue to be in effect, unless the upcoming regulations or the statute modifies them. I have attempted to refer to current regulations in areas that appear not to have been modified by the statute.

communication needs must be addressed. Some have interpreted these changes in the law (and I would agree) as challenging the *Rowley* interpretation of the IDEA and opening the way for a greater use of bilingual approaches to the education of deaf children (Pittman & Huefner, 2001).

The foundation for the improvement of educational results for deaf children therefore lies in the rejection of the ableist assumptions that surround their education. Deaf children can achieve at levels comparable to those of their hearing peers, not by ill-conceived attempts to minimize deafness but by recognizing that they optimally develop language manually and that a high level of ASL ability can serve as a basis for future educational progress. This is not to say that lipreading is not an important adaptive skill for deaf people in a hearing world; it is. However, as a method of language acquisition it is inefficient and ineffective for large numbers of deaf children. By allowing deaf children to be deaf and by building on their inherent strengths through the development of manual language, they will ultimately (and, some might think, paradoxically) be better able to compete in a hearing world.

## THE EDUCATION OF BLIND AND VISUALLY IMPAIRED CHILDREN

The bias schools have against Braille and their failure to teach it to blind and visually impaired students is another example of how ableist assumptions influence educational programs. In 1829, Louis Braille invented a revolutionary system of raised dots that enabled blind people to read. Yet, many blind and significantly visually impaired students are not benefiting from this old technology (Johnson, 1996). Though some attribute this to the rise of newer technologies such as taped books and voice synthesizers that may be making Braille obsolete (Shapiro, 1994), I believe the failure to teach blind children Braille is another example of ableism. Reading Braille is a disability-specific method of reading that many nondisabled parents and educators view as unacceptable. They often prefer that children with very low vision read print, even if this is inefficient, and that totally blind children listen to tapes. As one young person who has a significant vision disability said to me recently, "I was taught to read print, not Braille, because everyone felt it would make me more like sighted people." This despite the fact that reading print is difficult and exhausting for her.

The National Federation of the Blind (NFB), an advocacy organization of blind people, has taken a strong position favoring the teaching of Braille to blind children and those with other vision impairments:

> There's no substitute for Braille in taking notes, reading a speech, looking up words in a dictionary, studying a complicated text, or just having the fun of reading for yourself. Talk of forcing blind children to learn Braille shows the prejudice. Nobody talks of forcing sighted children to learn print. It is taken for granted as a right, a necessary part of education; so it should be with Braille and blind children. (National Federation of the Blind, n.d.)

Though some totally blind students do not learn Braille, the controversy around Braille often revolves around students with limited vision. Some students with vision impairments can learn to read print or can read print with accommodations such as large print. If these students have stable, nonprogressive vision conditions and can learn to read print efficiently, they should. However, when educators and parents insist that vision-impaired children read print to the exclusion of reading Braille, many visually impaired children remain functionally illiterate.

Another controversy regarding the education of blind children centers on whether schools are required to provide orientation and mobility services (O&M) to blind students under related services provisions of the IDEA. O&M teachers teach blind students how to get around using canes and other means. The goal of these services is to increase independence. It seems logical that if the goal of public education is to prepare students to function in the world, O&M would be a required component of the educational program of blind children. Though this seems logical, advocates for the blind complained to me when I worked as the director of

OSEP that they were having difficulty securing these services because the law at this time did not specifically name the service. Some have argued that school districts objected to providing these services due to cost, and this argument may have some merit. However, advocates pointed out that some of the same districts had hired full-time paraprofessionals to assist blind students, an expensive and, in the eyes of many disability activists, potentially harmful practice (Ferguson & Asch, 1989). Many advocates believe the schools would have been better off teaching these students to navigate on their own using O&M techniques.

Like the deaf community, the blind community has sought action by the federal government to address the shortcomings of the educational system. When the Clinton administration took office in 1993, representatives of the blind community successfully sought the issuance of a guidance similar to that issued concerning the education of deaf children. This guidance emphasized the importance of specialized services such as O&M and supported Braille instruction. When the IDEA was reauthorized in 1997, a requirement was added to mandate that when teams meet to develop IEPs for blind and visually impaired students, Braille must be considered. The reauthorized law also added O&M as a related service. It is hoped that these specific legal requirements will begin to change the ableist practices that have compromised the education of blind and visually impaired children.

## THE EDUCATION OF STUDENTS WITH LEARNING DISABILITIES

Blindness, deafness, and significant physical disability are relatively rare; their combined incidence is less than 1 percent of the total population of school-aged children (U.S. Department of Education, 2003). On the other hand, students with learning disabilities (LD) are common, about 5 percent of children. Although definitional arguments concerning the identification of these children abound (Lyon et al., 2001), educators have long recognized the phenomenon of children who seem intellectually able but have marked difficulty learning to read. This condition, commonly known as dyslexia, is by far the most frequent form of learning disability, affecting about 80 percent of the learning disability population (Lyon et al., 2001). Given its prevalence, one might think that these children would be less likely to be subjected to inappropriate ableist practices. However, the available evidence contradicts this assumption.

The National Longitudinal Transition Study (NLTS) investigated the educational results of a large sample of students with disabilities who attended high schools in the mid-1980s. (An updated version of this study is currently being conducted, and data are becoming available.) This study, the largest and most thorough of its kind, paints a less than satisfactory picture (Wagner et al., 1993). The NLTS, along with other data such as the performance of students with disabilities on statewide assessments and more recent research, confirms the fact that the educational attainment levels of students with learning disabilities is less than adequate. Students with learning disabilities drop out of school at relatively high rates—about twice that of nondisabled students (Wagner et al., 1993). These students also participate in higher education in relatively small numbers. The NLTS also documents the fact that relatively large numbers of these students are not taking challenging academic subjects. Given these findings, it might not be surprising that more recent data indicate that students with learning disabilities fail statewide assessments at alarming rates (Katzman, 2001).[3]

The reasons for the lack of acceptable educational outcomes for students with learning disabilities are complex. The main symptom of dyslexia is the failure to learn to read, and yet dyslexic children are not the only children who struggle with reading.

---

3. For the purpose of this chapter, I use the terms *learning disability* (LD) and *dyslexia* interchangeably for the following reasons. First, though the population of students with learning disabilities is diverse, a high percentage of children with learning disabilities have marked reading problems. Second, much of the research on LD is not categorized by type of LD. Finally, the way schools respond to dyslexia, in my view, is similar to the way they respond to other types of LD.

Therefore, ascribing the low level of achievement of many learning-disabled students to ableism alone is inappropriate: Some students' failure to learn to read may be due to poor instruction. However, there is evidence that ableist assumptions may still have a strong negative influence on the education of those children who struggle the most with learning to read.

Failure to learn to read has been of concern to educators and the general public for some time. Therefore, significant resources have been directed to the study of reading failure. In fact, early reading may be the most researched area of education. As schools implement standards-based reforms, educators are increasingly looking to research to help guide schools in improving their performance. To meet this need, the DOE contracted with the National Research Council (NRC) of the National Academy of Sciences to conduct a research synthesis in the area of early reading. The resulting book, *Preventing Reading Difficulties in Young Children* (Snow, 1998), was one of the biggest sellers at the NRC. As one party involved in the initial study design, the DOE insisted that the synthesis employ an inclusive design. The DOE considered this important because any inquiry into disabled children's failure to learn to read must be viewed in the overall context of how children learn to read. Conversely, given the relatively large number of students who have disabilities, the failure to address the needs of disabled students in a study of this magnitude would render the study noncomprehensive.[4] This study, therefore, contains a wealth of information about those students who have the most difficulty learning to read, including those likely to be dyslexic. Along with this study, more recent work published by researchers funded by the National Institutes of Health (NIH) provides a converging picture of how schools handle young students with dyslexia. Once the data from the NLTS and other sources have been added, the view through the ableist lens becomes most revealing.

---

4. More than 11 percent of students ages 6 to 17 received special education services during the 2000–01 school year (U.S. Department of Education, 2003).

Nevertheless, ableist assumptions may be impeding the effective education of children with disabilities. One example of this is the reluctance of some parents and teachers to intervene on behalf of children who are experiencing marked difficulty learning to read. Some of this reluctance may be due to a lack of appropriate options or inadequate teacher preparation (Lyon et al., 2001). However, some of the inaction may be due to schools' desire not to label children, which undoubtedly reflects the deep stigma associated with disability in our culture. The mere label of disability carries such negative connotations that many educators and some parents do their best to avoid it. Another reason that some may avoid labeling is the fact that a disability label may result in special education placements, which are often inferior to the regular classroom. These placements often reflect the ableist notion that disabled children should not be challenged; thus, some educators and parents justifiably avoid them. Finally, the federal definition of learning disability, which requires that a child exhibit a discrepancy between intelligence (IQ) and performance, may also inhibit early intervention. That is, the child must first fail to learn the material that his intelligence would indicate he should be able to learn before he can establish eligibility for special education services. From my perspective, the ethics of allowing young children to fail at learning to read without providing intensive help is questionable for all children, disabled and nondisabled.

The dilemma parents and educators face around the issue of labeling need not exist if schools employ research-based practices and improve their special education programs. The National Institutes of Health have conducted an extensive set of studies using large data sets that examine the nature of early reading failure. These studies have documented the fact that relatively large numbers of students experience significant difficulty with initial reading. There is evidence that of the 12 to 18 percent of the K–1 student population that has the most difficulty learning to read, research-based interventions are effective with 70 percent (Lyon et al., 2001). Though not all students fully benefit from these interventions, they can serve to identify students who are highly likely to need more extensive help, that is, those who may have a disability that will require accommodations and support throughout their schooling. These students are described in the literature as those who fail to respond to treatment of responsiveness to intervention (RTI) models of disability identification (Fuchs et al., 2004). Once it is clear that a child has not responded to powerful interventions and is still struggling with reading, that child should get the protections of the IDEA.

Though these "wait and fail" practices may have had a negative impact on the education of children with learning disabilities, there are opportunities for school districts to change this practice. The 2004 reauthorization of the IDEA does not require local education agencies (LEAs) to use the "severe discrepancy" model in determining eligibility for special education services for students with LD. The recent reauthorization also allows for the use of up to 15 percent of federal special education funds for, among other things, providing coordinated early intervention services in general education for students experiencing reading difficulties. It should also be noted that the 1997 reauthorization permitted schools to use the "developmental delay" eligibility category for students experiencing difficulty in school up to age eight. These provisions seem to be used increasingly by school districts. By the 2000–01 school year, 28,935 children were served under this designation—by far the fastest growing category of disability (U.S. Department of Education, 2003). All of these are hopeful signs that students with disabilities may get earlier, more appropriate interventions in the future. (The issue of early intervention for students with learning and behavioral difficulties will be dealt with more extensively in chapters 4 and 6.)

Another way ableist practices affect the achievement of students with learning disabilities is that their education tends to be inordinately oriented toward the presenting characteristics of the disability. Most dyslexic children are placed for part of the day in special education resource rooms and part of the day in regular classes (U.S. Department of Education, 2003). Some are in regular classes all day. For large numbers of these students, neither regular nor special class placements seem to be meeting their needs. Sharon Vaughn and her colleagues (2000) studied elementary schoolchildren with LD who were assigned to special classes and found that their instruction was characterized by large, multiaged groups and was largely nondifferentiated. Other studies have found that special education placement results in students reading less (Allington & McGill-Franzen, 1989). General classes did not do much better. NLTS documents show that a large number of students with LD who were placed in general education classrooms did not receive many accommodations or much support. Such students were more likely to fail and drop out of school. Another more recent study documented that 80 percent of the poorest readers placed in regular classrooms made no progress over an entire academic year (Klinger et al., cited in Lyon et al., 2001).

Students with dyslexia *can and do* learn to read. However, they need more intensive help to do so, and even with the best approaches they are likely to experience significant difficulty with reading, writing, and spelling throughout their schooling (Shaywitz, 2003; Torgesen, 2000; Torgesen et al., 2001). The picture that emerges from the research on remediation after grade two shows that reading improvement can continue but that those who have the most difficulty reading are likely to continue to have these problems and that their problems compound. Children with poor reading skills avoid reading and thus build up enormous educational deficits (Lyon et al., 2001). Given the centrality of reading to most instruction, severe reading problems can affect all areas of students' curricular attainment.

The research discussed thus far indicates several clear implications for educational practice. First, there is a population of children who are likely to experience significant difficulty with reading, even with the best interventions. Second, reading improvement for these students can continue throughout their schooling if that intervention is sufficiently intensive and appropriate. Third, those

with the most severe problems in reading print are likely to experience increasing difficulty in school as the cumulative effects
of reading deficiency become apparent. Fourth, significant numbers of these students are receiving inappropriate educational assistance in terms of both the interventions they receive and their
access to the curriculum.

Again, I believe that ableism at least partially explains our failure to better educate students with LD. As is the case with other
disabilities, programs for these students often focus on the characteristics of their disability—their reading deficiencies—to the exclusion of their overall educational needs. Like the deaf who must
learn to lip-read and speak before they can access the curriculum, it appears that many believe that those with LD must learn
to read at grade level before they can access other subjects. This
approach clearly magnifies the negative educational impact of the
disability.

This situation was brought home to me when I was associate superintendent of schools in Chicago in 1992. A general education
teacher asked to meet with me concerning students with LD in
her class. She told me that she was also a parent of a child with LD
and that she knew a good deal about the disability. She went on to
say that she had a number of students in her classes with LD who
were failing and that she had not been seen by anyone from the
special education department in her school. Later, a staff member
who worked with special education staff in the school informed
her that it was not their job to meet with the general education
teachers. These teachers viewed their responsibility as only working on the goals and objectives in the IEPs, which were largely dis-
crete skills centered on reading and writing. Therefore, students
with LD were being expected to handle text four and five grade
levels above their reading level without accommodation. No won-
der they were failing!

Can students with LD access curriculum above their reading level? Of course they can. However, for many of these students, that
access cannot be dependent on their ability to read print or write

at grade level. Therefore, focusing their special education program solely on learning to read is not appropriate. For students with LD, this reflects the ableist assumption that special education's role should be to overcome disabilities, even if that is not fully possible. Instead, these children must have the appropriate accommodations and supports to access the rest of the curriculum. Fortunately, there are accommodations available that can help students with LD access text written above their reading level. Taped books have been available to blind students for many years and are increasingly used by people with dyslexia. Recordings for the Blind recently changed its name to Recordings for the Blind and Dyslexic to reflect the changing demand for their services. Also, as more text is digitized, computers will be able to read text using screen readers. Other techniques, such as increasing students' ability to handle text by preteaching multisyllabic and technical words, can enable them to handle difficult texts more easily. Word processing and spell-checks can greatly enhance LD students' ability to produce writing assignments.

Although there are effective ways to help students with LD access the general education curriculum, schools may have to modify some deeply held beliefs about what constitutes acceptable student performance in order for these students to benefit from new technologies. In many schools, students are required to handle text at grade level or higher in order to be mainstreamed into regular classes. Taped books are not available or not allowed. Still other schools do not allow students to use computers when taking exams, thus greatly diminishing some students' ability to produce acceptable written work. Though some may defend this rigidity as a means to maintain standards, for students with LD this posture will likely lead to lower educational attainment.

The late disabilities advocate Ed Roberts had polio as a child, which left him with significant physical disabilities, including the need for an iron lung. He attended school from home in the 1960s with the assistance of a telephone link. When it was time for graduation, the school board was going to deny him a diploma because he had failed to meet the physical education requirement. His parents protested, and Ed eventually graduated (Shapiro, 1994). It would be difficult to imagine that happening today, given disability law and improved societal attitudes toward disability. Yet students with LD are still routinely required to read print at grade level to access educational opportunities, which reflects ableist assumptions. As the disability movement has demonstrated over and over, there is more than one way to walk, talk, paint, read, or write. Assuming otherwise is the root of fundamental inequities.

## STUDENTS WITH SERIOUS EMOTIONAL DISTURBANCE

No subpopulation of American students experiences poorer educational outcomes than those who have been identified as having serious emotional disturbance (SED). The NLTS has documented dismal results: Students with SED drop out of school at a rate of over 50 percent, and only 15.3 percent pursue higher education. The NLTS findings for students with such disabilities were so poor that the author of the study described them as "particularly troubling" (Wagner et al., 1991). These findings prompted changes in 1997 that, among other things, require students to be provided with appropriate behavioral supports and interventions and prohibit cessation of services for students who have been suspended or expelled from school.

The NLTS data also gave rise to serious concerns regarding the nature of these students' programs. For instance, only a small percentage received mental health or social work services, and few had their behavior addressed by their IEP. Data are available that show some significant progress since the original NLTS report on service delivery, indicating that approximately 50 percent of these students get behavior management services, up from 20 percent in the original study. Approximately the same number are receiving mental health services, again up from 20 percent. Social work services are provided to approximately 30 percent, up from 12 percent. Students with emotional disturbance continue to be segre-

gated in relatively large numbers, taking 44 percent of their courses in special education classes. This too is an improvement of 15
percent over the previous study. Other important findings in the
new study show that students with emotional disturbance continue to be identified later than other disability groups, on average at
age nine. Their parents also report significantly greater frustration
in getting their children served (Wagner & Cameto, 2004).

Although there is progress in certain areas for these students,
given their high levels of segregation (approximately 50%), it appears that treatment for large numbers of students with SED is
more focused on responding to the most common symptom of
their disability, acting-out behavior, than on providing the accommodations and support they need to succeed in school. This is
ableism in the extreme. One might assume that virtually all students with emotional disturbance, given the nature of their disability, might need counseling and mental health and social work
services. Further, given the fact that these children generally have
normal intelligence, the continued high levels of segregation raise
concerns over whether they have access to the curriculum. It appears that no group suffers from negative ableist attitudes more
than students with SED.

What do these children get from special education? A common
response to these children is to place them in a segregated special
classroom or a school with other children with similar disabilities.
The teacher is often uncertified. Only approximately 26 percent
of these students are integrated into regular education for 80 percent of their school day or more (U.S. Department of Education,
2003). There is ample evidence that placing these students in separate classes without attention to behavior, without counseling,
and with an uncertified teacher does not help them, while more
appropriate schoolwide behavior and prevention programs have
proven effective (Sugai et al., 2000). Given the data cited thus far,
we can seriously question whether many within this group are receiving the free and appropriate public education (FAPE) required

under the IDEA. (The issue of effective behavior supports will be addressed more extensively in chapter 4.)

In addition to limited access to the curriculum, these students face discriminatory discipline policies. The very nature of their disability, which is often accompanied by acting-out behavior, often puts these children at risk of removal or outright exclusion from school, particularly in an era of "zero tolerance" school discipline policies, whereby schools are often required to suspend or expel students for disciplinary offenses. Though the IDEA gives these students minimal protection, even these protections are fragile. Prior to the reauthorization in 1997, the DOE's interpretation that FAPE must be provided to all students, even those expelled from school, was challenged by the state of Virginia (Hehir, 2002). Though the state ultimately prevailed in court, the 1997 amendments rendered the decision moot by requiring states to make FAPE available to all students, even those expelled. Although these protections were a victory for these students, the issue of basic protection of access to education was not settled. The issue was revisited by Congress in the 2004 reauthorization, which allows school districts more discretion in removing students for disciplinary infractions. Fortunately, Congress retained the requirement to provide services to students with disabilities who have been suspended or expelled for more than ten days and retained (though redefined) protections for students whose offending behavior is the manifestation of a disability. (The issue of discipline and students with disabilities will be dealt with more extensively in chapters 4 and 6.)

Though some may argue that discipline policies should treat students with disabilities the same as nondisabled students, ignoring the impact a disability has on behavior can result in truly discriminatory, ableist practices. In many situations, a disability requires special accommodation, and false impartiality, or treating everybody the same, results in inequity (Minow, 1991). For example, allowing a person in a wheelchair "equal access" to a courthouse with stairs but no elevator is no access at all. Similarly, requiring emotionally disabled students to adhere to disciplinary policies without taking into account the impact of their disability is the equivalent of requiring students with mental retardation to perform academically at grade level without necessary supports. It is simply unreasonable and wrong, and it should continue to be illegal.

The issue of discipline and behavior is complex and emotionally charged. Most parents and educators expect schools to be orderly and that all children have the right to learn in a safe environment. Students with emotional disturbances need a safe and stable environment as well, but some of them need to be taught appropriate school behavior and be supported in achieving this goal. There is no evidence that punishing behavior that is the result of emotional disability will help the majority of such children to learn appropriate behavior and be able to function in school. There is, however, significant evidence that providing these students with appropriate supports and services in the context of schoolwide disciplinary policy can significantly reduce disruptive behavior and improve outcomes (Horner et al., 2000). This approach has also been demonstrated to improve disciplinary outcomes for all students. (A more thorough treatment of these approaches will appear in chapter 4.)

It is important to note that not all children with emotional disturbance exhibit "acting-out" behavior. Some may be exceptionally withdrawn and depressed. They too suffer from the negative societal attitudes associated with mental health disorders. Some of these students may also be placed in inappropriate segregated special education placements. I recall a phone call from a parent when I was special education director in Boston that brought this point home to me. The parent was concerned about her daughter's placement in a special education school after she had experienced a "breakdown." Prior to her placement in the special school, the girl had been in an academically challenging high school program. Her mother explained to me that they were poor African Americans living in a project and that she could not afford to send her daughter to a private school. She went on to say that her daughter had always loved school and books and that the special school she had been placed in had few books and was thus making her daughter more depressed. She pleaded with me to move her daughter back to her old high school.

I reviewed the file and noted that although the girl had a serious psychiatric disorder, with appropriate support and medication her prognosis was good. She was also gifted intellectually. After I met with the principal and various support and mental health personnel, a more appropriate plan was developed for this girl. She returned to her former high school, performed very well, and went on to a top-tier college. Though this story ended well, had it not been for an astute parent and receptive educators this girl may not have thrived, and the available evidence suggests that her successful program was the exception, not the rule. The response to this type of disability is often to "place" children in segregated programs rather than to develop individually tailored approaches that maximize the likelihood of success.

Children with emotional disturbances need not receive a poor education. Researchers and educators have developed approaches that greatly increase the likelihood that these children will be successful in their education and in life. These include early intervention for students experiencing marked behavioral difficulty (Walker et al., 1995); universally designed, schoolwide disciplinary and behavioral support (Sugai et al., 2000); and services that "wrap around" the child and the family (Eber & Keenan, 2004). For widespread change to occur, however, educators must first challenge their own ableist assumptions about these students. It is inappropriate to respond to these children simply by punishing them for their behavior, or by inappropriately removing them to segregated settings, or by assuming that these children's disability is their "fault." They need carefully constructed, individual programs that recognize the effects of their disability while seeking to create opportunities for them to learn and fully participate in school and society.

# 2

# Making the Right Educational Decisions for Students with Disabilities

Had they not believed in my inherent normality and potential, and had they not had the good fortune to meet professionals who also believed in the inherent normality of blind children, our relationship, my view of myself as a person who is among other things blind, my life would be totally different.

*—Adrienne Asch*

I hope the discussion of ableism so far has served to illustrate how the negative attitudes of society toward disability can vastly distort the education these children receive. However, simply identifying these injustices does little to correct them. Every day, parents and educators must make decisions concerning the education of these children. How much should my child be included? Should she have a full-time teacher's aide in the classroom? Should we focus on spelling this year? What about sending him to a special school where the staff has a great deal of expertise in his disability area? Should he have physical therapy, and where should it be performed? Should my child be educated within a community-based setting? How are we going to improve his ability to behave in an integrated setting? The answers to these questions can carry with them serious lifelong consequences.

Though it may be tempting to answer these questions by loading up the individualized education program (IEP) with every possible service and try to do it all, children in general and children with disabilities in particular often need focused attention in order to learn most effectively. For some students more can be less. As Sally Shaywitz (2003) emphasizes, dyslexic children need programs that maximize their strengths and minimize their weaknesses. Therefore, she recommends that these children limit the number of courses they take with high reading content and that they have significantly modified foreign language instruction: "This is a very useful accommodation. Furthermore, it prevents needless suffering and waste of a student's time and energy while allowing him to focus on courses that he has a real chance of mastering" (Shaywitz, 2003, p. 319). In addition, school districts have finite resources, and it is unreasonable to expect them to fund an array of services that may not be justified or may even be counterproductive.

The lens of eliminating ableism becomes a helpful tool in assisting parents and educators to make these difficult decisions. First, an understanding of ableism should sensitize people about the role education often plays in reproducing social inequity. Much has been written, particularly by sociologists, about how education often reproduces social inequity for racial and linguistic minorities. However, relatively little has been written concerning how schools may do the same for those with disabilities. As the previous chapter's discussion made clear, the same inequity often occurs for students with disabilities. Inordinate segregation, low expectations, failure to provide accommodations, and misguided attempts to "cure" disability are all examples of practices that serve to keep disabled students in a subordinate position. Further, inappropriate placement of racial minorities in special education classrooms is often cited by these same scholars as the vehicle by which schools prevent racial minorities from achieving equity

(Losen & Orfield, 2002). Special education should reject that role. The goal of education for students with disabilities should not be to reinforce the status quo but rather to serve as a vehicle for equity and empowerment of disabled people. The decisions made every day at IEP meetings should serve that goal.

The lens of ableism may reveal distortions that often impact the education of children with disabilities when the goal is to "cure" or inappropriately reduce the "symptomatology" of disability. Harlyn Rousso (1984), an accomplished psychologist with cerebral palsy, recounts her mother's attempts to get her to walk "normally":

> My mother was quite concerned with the awkwardness of my walk. Not only did it periodically cause me to fall but it made me stand out, appear conspicuously different—which she feared would subject me to endless teasing and rejection. To some extent it did. She made numerous attempts over the years of my childhood to have me go to physical therapy and to practice walking "normally" at home. I vehemently refused her efforts. She could not understand why I would not walk straight. (p. 9)

This sort of practice still goes on every day in schools. This is not only wasteful but may communicate the wrong message to children about their disabilities. Rousso goes on:

> Now I realize why. My disability, with my different walk and talk and my involuntary movements, having been with me all my life, was part of me, part of my identity. With these disability features I felt whole. My mother's attempt to change my walk, strange as it may seem, felt like an assault on myself, an incomplete acceptance of me, an attempt to make me over. I fought back because I wanted to be accepted as I was. (p. 9)

The provision of services that inordinately seek to "cure" disability is not only potentially harmful to the child's self-image and thus a waste of resources but may be harmful to the child's education by pulling him out of important academic education. One common practice in providing special education services is to remove the child from general education classes for part of the day to provide special services. Though this may be justified, care must be given to make sure that the provision of these services does not compromise the child's education. This point was illustrated for me during a training session I conducted for parents of students with disabilities. During the session a parent approached me about the failure of his son's school district to provide him with physical therapy. He described his son as having cerebral palsy (CP) and as a middle school–aged boy with above average intelligence. I asked the dad why his son needed physical therapy. He responded, "Because he has CP!" After further discussion it became clear that the father was not sure whether there was a reasonable expectation that the provision of physical therapy would result in his son being able to walk. I further asked this man if he knew what the child might be pulled out of in order to get physical therapy. He did not know. I responded that it was likely that his son would use his brain rather than his body to make a living in the future and that if the therapy sessions resulted in his being pulled out of a major subject, such as math, his future aspirations might be compromised. The boy's father thanked me and said that he had never thought of the issues I had raised. This father was doing what he felt was in the best interests of his son by advocating for what he perceived to be his son's needs. Indeed, the child may have needed physical therapy. I had no way to judge that with the information provided. However, I was sure that he also needed to get a solid education.

Meeting the specific needs that may arise out of a child's disability should not compromise educational goals. Had there been a strong justification for the physical therapy for this young boy beyond a perceived relationship between the service and the symptomatology of the disability, physical therapy sessions could have taken place after school or at a time that would not interrupt his academic education. To me, the worrisome aspect of this conversation was that nobody appeared to have discussed these important issues with the father, even though the child must have had numerous IEP meetings by this time. Employing the lens of ableism would have naturally led to these questions and would have resulted in better educational decision making for this child.

Another positive aspect of the lens of eliminating ableism is that it situates the education of children with disabilities within a broader school and societal context of disability rights. Again, a major tenet of the disability rights movement is that the way in which society responds to disability is more important than changing the individual with a disability (Shapiro, 1994). In environments where people sign, deafness is not disabling. Buildings that are ramped allow people who use wheelchairs equal access. In these environments the deaf do not have to learn to lip-read, and those with physical disabilities do not have to learn to walk in order to participate in society. This thinking has given rise to the concept of universal design, which will be discussed at length in chapter 4. Often in schools, however, the onus for participation is placed on the child. That is, the child must perform at a particular academic level or behave in an acceptable way to access appropriate education. For instance, children with dyslexia must be able to handle texts that are far above their reading level in order to access content areas, while autistic children must behave in a typical fashion to be included in general education. These types of expectations may not be possible for the child, and the subsequent denial of educational opportunity is thus clearly inappropriate.

Douglas Biklen (1992), in *Schooling without Labels,* constructed narratives of some of the first parents of students with significant developmental disabilities who sought school inclusion for their children during the eighties. These parents encountered numerous barriers to their children's integration. Prominent among them were what Biklen referred to as the "myth of clinical judgment." He described this practice:

> Special Educators usually describe their work as clinical. They treat individuals. In their work with groups, they nevertheless attempt to individualize their "interventions." They are presumed to possess current expert knowledge. And they are expected to exert professional judgment in each case they handle. They recommend

and sometimes have the power to require a particular treatment. (Biklen, 1992, p. 83)

The children in Biklen's study all had very significant disabilities, and their functioning levels would likely always deviate from the norm regardless of what interventions were provided. The unwillingness, due to the level of these children's disabilities, of some school officials to provide them with important developmental opportunities and the hope of a semblance of a regular life was, in the eyes of these visionary parents, discriminatory and unjust.

The parents in Biklen's study often were in a position where they challenged the power of clinical judgment when, in their view, it limited the options for their children or underestimated their children's potential. One set of parents, Rose and Dom Galati, expressed this frustration: "I'll be damned if the education system is going to work diametrically opposed to me. I can't believe that people would say to a parent, 'I'm sorry but the system isn't ready for you'" (Biklen, 1992, p. 6). Biklen continued:

> Naturally, some parents ask: Is it right for the states' experts to have sole authority to determine what is "appropriate" for people with disabilities? Should courts and society defer to state experts to decide whether to institutionalize a child, or segregate students with disabilities into separate schools or decide whether a child shall be physically restrained or punished in the name of treatment? We might ask other questions. Should any child, or for that matter, any adult be institutionalized for reasons of disabilities? Should school districts separate any students from regular schools and classes? In defending themselves against such forced segregation, should people with disabilities and their own experts have less authority than state experts? (p. 98)

I frequently meet parents who continue to struggle with these issues. Eliminating ableism will require schools to examine their practices and to recognize their responsibility to provide accessible educational environments that enable disabled students to participate and be educated to their true potential.

## THE GOAL AND PURPOSE OF SPECIAL EDUCATION

If we accept the presumption that students with disabilities have a right to participate in general education and be educated to their true potential, then a logical question that arises is the role of special education in achieving that goal. Though some disability activists react negatively to the very use of the term "special," as a practical reality special education is the vehicle by which we have constructed the support that many students with disabilities need to be successful in school. Special education is a major component of American education, federally mandated through the Individuals with Disabilities Education Act (IDEA), with strong support from parents and most educators. The strong bipartisan support this legislation receives when periodic reauthorizations occur is evidence of this support. Yet there appears to be considerable confusion concerning special education's role in this era of inclusive education and standards-based reform.

I am frequently asked to conduct workshops for school personnel from both general education and special education. Lately, I have been asking participants to spend a few minutes with another member of their cohort and consider the following question: "What should the purpose of special education or the education of students with disabilities be?" Common responses include "meeting the goals on children's IEPs," "meeting the needs of disabled students," "helping all children who are struggling in school," "returning children to regular education," "the same as general education," "enabling children to reach their full potential," "providing children with disabilities with access to the curriculum." Though there is merit in each of these responses, from my perspective several are problematic, and all evidence significant goal confusion regarding the role of special education in American schools.

Those who seek to meet the goals identified in IEPs must first make sure those goals are appropriate and do not represent low or unrealistic goals for students. Further, reducing education to the goals on IEPs does not, in my view, reflect a robust view of education. Returning children to regular education is particularly problematic on several levels. First, such a statement may be interpreted to mean that the provision of special education services assumes removal. This flies in the face of the least restrictive environment (LRE) requirements and inclusive practice. Also, this statement seems to assume that special education has interventions powerful enough to "cure" or significantly reduce the symptomatology of disability. There is no evidence that such practices exist for the vast majority of students with disabilities (Hocutt, 1996). Most experts agree that dyslexia, the most common disability served by special education, is a lifelong disability (Shaywitz, 2003). The notion of special education as a support to all struggling students immediately raises concerns about racial equity issues, given the troubled history of the overrepresentation of minorities in special education classes (Losen & Orfield, 2002). Though responses such as "the same as regular education" or "providing access to the general education curriculum" may seem compatible with the goal of eliminating ableism in that they evidence integrationist intent and high expectations, they may be a bit too simplistic. For instance, many school districts have the goal that all children meet "high academic standards," with success being measured by performance on standardized tests or rates of college admittance. How do children with significant mental retardation fit into that goal? Also, if the curriculum provided by the district is rigid and narrow, it may not allow students to learn important skills relevant to independence that nondisabled students may already have, like crossing streets or making purchases in stores.

What, then, should the role of special education be? I have struggled with this issue and have found guidance in the narratives of adults with disabilities and those of parents of children with disabilities. These narratives are rich and varied and span several decades. Noteworthy among them is the work of Adrienne Asch, a blind woman who teaches at Wellesley College. Asch analyzed various narratives of adults with disabilities about their experiences as children and identified themes that emerged concerning the way in which their parents and educators responded to their disability. One common response was to overreact to disability with excessive concern and sheltering. Asch theorizes that this response is underrepresented in narratives because individuals who experience this type of upbringing do not have the sense of personal empowerment required to write narratives. Another common reaction to disability conveyed to children was that nothing was "wrong." This was communicated to these children through parental silence or denial. One narrative relates how a young woman with significant vision loss was not given any alternative but to use her limited vision even though she experienced significant academic problems as a result. Another common theme was the ill-conceived attempts to fix disability. Rousso's (1984) description of how her mother tried to change her "walk" is an example of this type of narrative. Asch, recalling her own upbringing and education, describes a more positive response to disability. Her parents and teachers minimized the impact of her disability while making sure that she led a full life.

> In thinking about the writing of disabled adults and reflecting on my own life, I give my parents high marks. They did not deny that I was blind, and did not ask me to pretend that everything about my life was fine. They rarely sheltered. They worked to help me behave and look the way others did without giving me a sense that to be blind—"different"—was shameful. They fought for me, to ensure that I lived as full and rich a life as I could. For them, and consequently for me, my blindness was a fact, not a tragedy. It affected them but did not dominate their lives. Nor did it dominate mine. (Ferguson & Asch, 1989, p. 118)

I believe that Asch's narrative and the narratives of parents in Biklen's work provide useful guidance for defining the purpose of special education. I believe the role of special education should be *to minimize the impact of disability and maximize the opportunities for children with disabilities to participate in general education in their natural community.* This framework assumes that most children with disabilities will be integrated into general education and be educated within their natural community, with special education serving as a vehicle for access and addressing the specific needs that arise out of children's disabilities.

This framework—minimizing the impact of disability while maximizing a child's ability to participate—explicitly acknowledges that "differences" that arise out of childhood disability matter and therefore avoids the pitfalls of what Martha Minow (1991) refers to as impartiality or what some disability activists would consider denial. "Through deliberate attention to our own partiality, we acknowledge the dangers of pretended impartiality. By taking difference into account, we can overcome our pretended indifference to difference and our tendency to sort the world into same and different" (Minow, 1991, p. 389). In order to determine the impact of disability we first must acknowledge its existence and then determine what should be done to minimize its impact. Thus, this articulation of the purpose of special education implicitly rejects the role special education has at times served in promoting inordinate segregation, low expectations, and overprotection. These practices are inconsistent with the purposes of minimizing the impact of disabilities and fostering participation.

This framework is also consistent with the IDEA. Prior to the 1997 reauthorization the IDEA was vague in its definition of special education as "specialized designed instruction to meet the unique needs of a child with a disability." The 1997 amendments clarified this vagueness by requiring that IEP teams address how a child will access the curriculum as well as meet the unique needs that may arise out of that child's disability (IDEA 1997, 300.26). This legal clarification provides a safeguard against children being denied access while acknowledging the importance of a child's specific disability. These provisions, coupled with the long-standing requirement that children be educated in the least restrictive environment, support the overall goal of integrating children with disabilities into their school and their community.

Finally, defining the role of special education as minimizing the impact of disability and maximizing opportunities to participate provides a framework that can embrace the diverse needs that arise out of various disabilities as well as the individual diversity found among children within disability groups. Disabled children are a highly diverse group of children with widely varying needs (McDonnell et al., 1997). Therefore, narrow policies aimed at a particular population may not serve another population. This truth was illuminated by the debate that raged within special education over the past fifteen years over the issue of full inclusion. Though it would be difficult to argue that the children portrayed in Biklen's book did not benefit from school and community integration, many within the disability community believed that full inclusion would compromise the interests of other groups of disabled children. How, for instance, would the high school student with dyslexia be able to receive intense specialized instruction in reading if he could never be removed from a general education class? The issue of inclusive schooling and its relationship to eliminating ableism will be discussed at length in the next chapter. Suffice it to say at this point that the proposed purpose of special education allows for diversity in the populations served as well as the approaches pursued, as the following examples show.

### Minimizing the Impact of Disability

Minimizing the impact of disability, as Asch's narrative attests, does not involve misguided attempts to cure disability but rather involves giving children the skills and opportunities they need to live as full a life as possible with their disability. In Asch's case that meant learning Braille as well as orientation and mobility skills and having appropriate accommodations available that enabled her to access education. Special education thus provided her with the necessary means of access that minimized the impact of her disability. An important point that Asch makes, referring to the work of Wright (1983), is that in her case the "spread" of her disability was also minimized. That is, she and her family were not required to disrupt their lives in order to receive the specialized services she needed. She could live at home and attend her local school because of the enlightened policies of New Jersey at the time. Unfortunately, even today, many parents of "low-incidence" disabled students such as the blind and the deaf are not afforded the opportunity Asch was in the early 1950s. They are faced with the choice of sending their children to local schools that are ill equipped to meet their needs or to a residential school with the specialized services their children need. For most this is no choice at all. On the one hand, at a local school their children will not get the services they need to access education. On the other, sending a very young child off to a residential school disrupts normal family life. This is a Hobson's choice that parents should not be forced to make. Certainly, it has been demonstrated that services for blind children can be provided in typical community settings and that most students can thrive in that environment. It is up to educators and policy makers to assure that such services are available.

The issues concerning the education of deaf children illustrate how minimizing the impact of disability might play out as a purpose of special education. As the discussion in the first chapter should have made clear, the issues involved in the education of deaf children are complex, given the impact of deafness on language development and the central role language plays in educational attainment. To reiterate a central point of that discussion, the language development of deaf children of deaf parents demonstrates that the impact of deafness can be minimized with appropriate approaches to early language development. However, relatively few deaf children have deaf parents, approximately 10 percent (Lane, in Kauffman & Hallahan, 1995). Therefore, deaf infants and toddlers should have intensive early intervention services around language acquisition, preferably through manual approaches. Further, parents and family members should learn manual language in order to maximize language development. In my opinion this should happen even for children with cochlear implants, given the importance of early language development and the fact that learning to sign has no demonstrated deleterious impact for deaf or hearing children. The deck should be stacked in favor of maximal language development. As deaf children move toward preschool and beyond, lipreading and learning standard English should be components of their education if we accept the goal of minimizing the impact of disability. Although lipreading is an imperfect means for most deaf people to access oral communication, being able to lip-read is an important tool for deaf people to have when American Sign Language (ASL) interpreters are not available. High levels of literacy in standard English are necessary to access higher levels of education.

Given the complexity of needs that arise out of deafness and its relatively low incidence, less than one per 1,000 children (U.S. Department of Education, 2003), the model of service delivery of bringing services to the individual child may be less feasible and possibly less desirable for many deaf children. First, though we would like to have all deaf children begin kindergarten with comparable vocabularies to hearing children, unless there is a sea change in the preschool experiences of deaf children, a minority of deaf kindergartners will attain this level of language development. Therefore, schools will have to continue to provide intensive language development opportunities, and the optimal way this may occur for some children is within classes with other deaf children taught by highly skilled teachers of the deaf. Therefore, programs with a critical mass of deaf students or schools for the deaf may be the most effective option for many deaf students.

The narratives collected by Biklen (1992) from parents whose children have significant developmental disabilities also illustrate the importance of minimizing the focus on the impact of disability. These narratives demonstrate the phenomenon of the spread of disability, whereby the presence of a significant disability in a child precluded the development of that child's relationships with other children within the community, thus maximizing the impact of the disability. Fortunately, these parents intuitively understand the deleterious impact that segregation had on their children and their family. Their successful efforts to provide integration for their children demonstrated the remedy for the spread of disability and thus minimized its impact.

The parents of these children with very significant disabilities challenged powerful societal forces that in their minds were limiting their children's options without any obvious benefit. Beginning with the birth of their children, the pressures to institutionalize and segregate were intense on these families. Intuitively, these parents saw no benefit for their children deriving from these practices. Mary Lou Accetta, who adopted a young boy, Melvin, who had been institutionalized, captures this instinctual reaction: "I always had the sense that there was a bright little kid under there. He was reacting so strongly to his environment." After relating how Melvin would act violently when she returned him to the institution after spending weekends at Mary Lou's, she concluded, "You're right; you shouldn't be here" (Biklen, 1992, p. 24). Mary Lou adopted Melvin, who was later included in school and made enormous progress both socially and academically. Melvin's case study speaks volumes about both the misguided policies of segregation and institutionalization as well as the benefits of creating opportunities in which children with disabilities can thrive within their schools and communities. Melvin went from an institutional placement that maximized the impact of his disability to one in which he was included in a family, a school, and a community, an environment that minimized the impact of his disability. He went from being a violent, unhappy child to a happy child who did well in school and made friends in his community.

The initial societal response to the children's disabilities in Biklen's study was, in short, to maximize the impact of disability. Institutionalization removed these children from loving families, while segregated education precluded the benefits of typical role models and friendships with children in the community. All the parents in Biklen's study independently came to the conclusion that segregation harmed their children and that integration was a necessary condition for their children to thrive. Instinctively, they knew what would minimize the impact of their children's disabilities even if the professionals did not. The dominant response of society to institutionalize and segregate children with significant cognitive disabilities, though significantly lessened, continues today. However, if special education embraces its role in minimizing the impact of disability, then institutionalization and segregation will be viewed as highly questionable practices for students with significant cognitive disabilities.

## Maximizing Opportunities to Participate

First and foremost, maximizing opportunities to participate in society is greatly enhanced when children are provided with a quality education. And, as previously mentioned in chapter 1, current educational outcomes for students with disabilities are unacceptable for large numbers of students with disabilities. Therefore, the remainder of this volume is devoted to improving educational opportunities for students with disabilities.

Public schools long ago adopted a role that goes beyond improving students' academic learning. Sports teams, choruses, clubs, and field trips are all fixtures of American education that provide significant benefit to children. Children who participate in these activities develop friendships, learn important skills, and cultivate leisure interests that enrich their lives. The importance of these activities has been recognized within the research. The National Longitudinal Transition Study (NLTS) found that students with disabilities who belonged to organized groups had lower absenteeism, a lower probability of course failure, and a reduced likelihood of dropping out of school, holding a number of other factors constant (Wagner et al., 1991). Again, Asch's narrative testifies to the importance of full participation to her childhood experience: "For me participating meant joining the chorus, the drama club, writing and debating groups. It meant not being excluded from after-school activities and class trips by teachers, club leaders, or the transportation system" (Ferguson & Asch, 1989, p. 129).

Though few would debate the importance of participation in these types of activities, there continue to be barriers to full participation of students with disabilities in all aspects of school and community life. Parents of students who do not attend their home schools complain that their children's participation in extracurricular activities is often at the mercy of bus schedules. Discrimination still looms large in the lives of many children with disabilities. Again, as I write this chapter, the local television station is reporting about the exclusion of a child with autism from his school's playground. His parents are challenging this action in court. His attorney stated that the child's participation on the playground was part of his special education program, reflecting the importance of full participation for this child.

Beyond assuring access to typical extracurricular activities, schools may have to play an enhanced role in providing disabled children with opportunities to participate. Special education law implicitly recognizes this need with its transition requirements.[1]

It is important to note at this point in the discussion that individual children's needs vary greatly even within the same disability population and at different stages of their development. The illustrations given thus far are not meant to imply that the same type of program is appropriate for each child with the same disability. For instance, the deaf child who comes to school with well-developed language may be able to be served effectively within his local school and thus will not need to be placed in a program or school for the deaf. Some children with mental retardation may need to spend more time within a community-based setting when

---

1. For children 14 and over, the IDEA requires schools to do transition planning, which is defined as a coordinated set of activities that is designed to promote movement from school to postschool activities, including postsecondary education and employment (IDEA 1997, 200.2d).

they reach adolescence than they did when they were in elementary school, where they may have been fully included in general education classes (Brown et al., 1991). The point of this discussion is to show the utility of defining special education's purpose of minimizing the impact of disability and maximizing the opportunities to participate as well as the applicability of this framework to all children with disabilities.

## INTERVENTIONS AND ACCESS

The important decisions that parents and school personnel make at IEP meetings can and should have long-term consequences for children, their families, and the educators who serve them. Basically, these decisions can be thought of in two types: decisions around interventions and decisions concerning access. Carefully made, these decisions should have as their goal minimizing the impact of disability and maximizing opportunities to participate.

For the purpose of this decision-making framework I define interventions as services designed to respond to needs that arise out of disability while minimizing the impact of the disability. However, it is important to reiterate here that for most students with disabilities interventions do not eliminate the impacts of disability but lessen them (Hocutt, 1996). For most students with disabilities IEP decisions involve interventions, and these interventions can have a major impact on the students' educational prospects both positively and negatively. Teaching a blind child to read Braille, providing intensive specialized help to a dyslexic student to help her break the phonetic code, assisting a child with articulation problems to learn to speak more clearly, intervening early in the lives of children with autism through structured behavioral therapies, teaching a student how to transfer from his wheelchair to a classroom chair are a few examples of common interventions that can greatly reduce the impact of disability. Therefore, the consideration of appropriate interventions should be a major focus at many if not most IEP meetings.

However, inappropriate interventions can exacerbate the impact of disability. As the children described by Biklen demonstrate, the once-common intervention response to significant cognitive disability, to institutionalize, would have maximized the impact of their disability by separating them from their families and the developmental opportunities available only in integrated environments. Though this illustrates the extreme, other interventions can have subtle yet deleterious effects on children. Narratives such as Rousso's speak to this. Further, some interventions involve removal from regular education classes and therefore can result in serious trade-offs.

Access decisions involve providing children with opportunities to participate in regular classrooms and activities. Such decisions are central to goals of minimizing impact and maximizing opportunities to participate. Narratives of adults with disabilities speak to the wisdom of promoting access. However, as is the case with intervention, decisions around access can either promote or work against the attainment of educational opportunity. A child with dyslexia who is integrated into a regular education class without accommodations for his reading disability is likely to have great difficulty gaining access to the material and thus experience educational failure. The child with cognitive disabilities who gains access to a regular classroom through the provision of a one-on-one aide may develop inordinate dependencies.

The critical decisions regarding interventions and access are a major focus of this book and are dealt with at length in the forthcoming chapters.

## IMPORTANT CONSIDERATIONS IN SPECIAL EDUCATION DECISIONMAKING

### 1. Differential diagnosis is important.

Though the mere use of the term *differential diagnosis* conjures up the return to the "medical model" of disability that many in the field have rightfully criticized (Biklen, 1992), in order to minimize the impact of disability parents and educators need to have a clear understanding of the nature of the child's disability. For instance, a third grader may not be reading well for a variety of reasons that are relevant to decision making. For instance, the child may not be reading well due to mental retardation, dyslexia, a hearing impairment, or attention difficulties. Knowing why a child is having difficulty is central to good educational decisions. The child with mental retardation, though behind, may be reading at his reading expectancy level, which would indicate that the current approach is working well, whereas the child with attention problems may need targeted accommodations or carefully prescribed medication. The student with dyslexia may need a highly structured reading program provided by a teacher with specialized training, while the child with a hearing impairment may need a new hearing aid. Another example that illustrates this point involves two vision-impaired children who are learning to read via large print and have the same visual acuity level. Their vision condition may be central to the decision of whether to teach them Braille. One may have a stable condition, while the other may have a progressive condition with the high likelihood of deteriorating vision with age. Though the student with the progressive condition may be functioning well today, teaching him Braille now may be important to assure his success in the future.

### 2. *Consider family capacity and desires.*

Parents are children's first teachers, and making good educational decisions should take into account family capacity and desires. This point was brought home to me during a discussion I had with the parent of an adolescent with Down's syndrome. In discussing her son's high school program, she said, "I don't want the school wasting his time learning to cook or do laundry. I can do that! As a matter of fact, he is already a pretty good cook. I want him in band class." Though many believe that learning independent living skills is important for many children, particularly those with mental retardation, learning to cook would be a waste of precious instructional time for this boy. His family was already doing a great deal to minimize the impact of his disability. This is the partnership all educators should seek with parents.

Beyond considering family capacity and desires, educators should be working with families to ally them in the schools' efforts to minimize the impact of disability. I recently had a discussion with a deaf woman at a professional conference who underscored the benefits of this approach. This woman was a lawyer who had been born deaf and had deaf parents. She was currently filling a significant administrative role in higher education, with many staff reporting to her. She clearly had attained high levels of language and literacy. I asked her, given her deafness, how that happened? She said she credited her parents, who, from the time she and her deaf sister were young, emphasized language and literacy. She said her parents were voracious readers and that her home was full of books and magazines. Clearly, parents and schools working together to minimize disability and maximize participation provide the greatest hope for a bright future.

### 3. Involve students with disabilities in educational decisions where appropriate.

Just as parents are critical in achieving better results, so are students. Students can provide important insights about the impact of their disability and the most effective way in which they learn. It is also important for students, particularly as they move into adolescence, to take appropriate responsibility for their own education. Further, students with disabilities need to understand both the nature and impact of their own disability if they are going to be able to advocate for themselves as they move into higher education and employment. Finally, students need to integrate their disability into their self-image in a way that is natural and positive (Rousso, 1984). For all of these reasons there has been significant attention in the field to self-determination, particularly for adolescents. Self-determination is the opposite of the paternalism that plagued the lives of so many people with disabilities. Many in the field have promoted the concept of self-determination as a vehicle to assist adolescents with disabilities in making a successful transition to adulthood (Ward, 1988). Central to this concept is the empowerment of youth to express their own needs and interests and to take increased responsibility for their future (Holub, Lamb, & Bang, in Jorgensen, 1997). In order for students to take this responsibility, they must have a deep understanding of their disability and its impact.

In her book, *Restructuring High Schools for All Students: Taking Inclusion to the Next Level,* Jorgensen (1997) provides practical suggestions about how to involve students in the decisions that impact their education as well as rich narratives of students that demonstrate the value of this approach. One student captured the importance of this approach. After initially reacting negatively about discussing her disability in a self-determination class, Natasha, a student who was struggling in school, stated, "If a teacher told me to do extra credit work or anything on my own, I'd usually forget it. But once I did a couple of activities [from the self-determination curriculum], I realized I wasn't doing them for the teacher. I was doing them for me. I liked owning my life" (Jorgensen, 1997, p. 203)

During the signing ceremony for IDEA 1997, Judy Heumann exhorted students with disabilities: "We can open doors for you, but it won't mean a thing if you don't study hard. . . . Join with your nondisabled classmates and build America's accessible house!"

### 4. Encourage disabled students to develop and use skills and modes of expression that are most effective and efficient for them.

This book has sought to demonstrate that the strong preference within society, reflected in school practice, to have disabled students perform in the same way that nondisabled children perform can ultimately be handicapping for some students. This is not to say that it is not desirable for disabled students to be able to perform in the way nondisabled students perform. For instance, deaf students who can read lips have a competitive advantage in a hearing world. However, assuming that most deaf children can develop elaborate language through oral methods has been proven false, and employing these methods without allowing for the natural development of language almost assures poor language development. What may appear to be a paradox to some is that a deaf child who has well-developed language through learning ASL from birth may actually have a higher likelihood of reading lips because he simply has a larger vocabulary. The problem is not, therefore, in the natural desire of parents and educators to have children be able to perform in a typical manner but, rather, the missed educational opportunities many disabled students experience because of a lack of regard for what are often disability-specific modes of learning and expression. This issue will be explored more in chapter 4, which deals with the issue of universal design.

### 5. The importance of integration into general education environments should be a central consideration.

If the purpose of special education is to minimize the impact of disability and maximize the ability to participate, then the importance of integration in schooling is obvious. Integration is associated with better educational results (Wagner et al., 1993). Also, if our goal is to give all children a quality education that will enable them to lead full lives within the community, for most children integration will be a necessary condition to achieve that result. However, there are times when this goal cannot be achieved optimally in a general education environment. The issue of integration is such an important and complex one that the next chapter is devoted to this issue. It proposes a framework to help educators and parents make intervention and access decisions.

### 6. Promote high standards.

An important point to reiterate here is that the most damaging ableist assumption is the belief that disabled people are incapable. Therefore, the movement to include students with disabilities in standards-based reforms holds promise. However, high-stakes testing that prevents students from being promoted or from receiving a diploma based on performance on standardized tests is problematic on a number of levels. A promising movement, standards-based reform, may ultimately reinforce current inequities if performance on high-stakes tests becomes the only means by which disabled students can demonstrate what they know and are able to do. Chapter 5 provides an in-depth discussion of the centrality of standards-based reform to current education policy and the complexities of including students with disabilities in these accountability systems.

### 7. Apply concepts of universal design to schooling.

A principle of disability policy that has evolved is the concept of universal design. First applied to architecture, this principle called for the design of buildings with the assumption that people with disabilities would be using them. With the legal backing of the Americans with Disabilities Act, these principles are applied increasingly to new construction and renovation of public buildings. Ramps, automatic door-opening devices, accessible toilets, and fire alarm systems with lights activated for the deaf are examples of universal design features incorporated into contemporary buildings. Other examples extend to technologies. Captioning devices are required features on all televisions, and digital text can be read from computers with screen readers. Universal design allows for access without extraordinary means and is based on the assumption that disabled people are numerous and should be able to lead regular lives. In short, universal design minimizes the impact of disability. These principles have recently been applied to schooling and show tremendous promise. Given the importance of these recent innovations and their potential to greatly improve the education of children with disabilities, chapter 4 is devoted to this issue.

# 3

# Inclusive Education

The movement to include greater numbers of students with disabilities, particularly those with significant cognitive disabilities, in regular education classes has had a profound effect on the education of students with disabilities. Over the past decade, more and more students with disabilities have been educated for more of the day in regular education classrooms. In the most recent year for which data are available, approximately 45 percent of students with disabilities were educated in regular classes up to 80 percent of their day. An additional 38 percent of students with disabilities were educated from 40 percent to 79 percent in regular classes. Thus, up to 83 percent of children with disabilities spend a significant amount of their day in regular classes (U.S. Department of Education, 2003).

The inclusion movement in education has supported the overall disability movement's goal of promoting societal integration, using integration in schooling as a means to achieve this result. In 1977 disability activists took over federal offices in San Francisco for twenty-five days, demanding that regulations for implementing

Section 504 of the Rehabilitation Act, the first federal act to broadly ban discrimination based on disability, be released. The protesters were particularly concerned about leaked draft regulations that provided for separate segregated education for disabled students. Judy Heumann, one of these protesters, stated, "We will accept no more segregation" (Shapiro, 1994). The final rules were revised to encourage integration in schooling, and the newly passed PL 94-142 (later renamed the Individuals with Disabilities Education Act, or IDEA) incorporated the current requirement that children be educated in the least restrictive environment (i.e., in regular classes as much as is appropriate for the child).

The strong legal preference for placement in regular classes, coupled with the political movement of disability activists and parents, has resulted in significant positive change for students with disabilities, who are moving on to jobs and accessing higher education at unprecedented levels (Hehir & Gamm, 1999). Virtually every school has had to confront the issue of inclusion as parents seek integration for their children with disabilities. However, like all change movements, inclusion has encountered opposition. Some opposition has reflected deeply held negative attitudes toward people with disabilities similar to those experienced by Joe Ford when his mother, Penny, enrolled him in first grade. I can recall a principal challenging me in a large public meeting concerning our efforts to promote inclusion in Chicago: "You don't really mean students who drool in regular classes?"

Many general education organizations representing educators have taken positions on the issue through position papers and resolutions. An example of this is the American Federation of Teachers: "Resolved that the AFT oppose inclusion—that is, any movement or program that has the goal of placing all students with disabilities in general education classrooms regardless of the nature or severity of their disabilities, their ability to behave or function appropriately in the classroom, or the educational benefits they and their general education peers can derive" (Kauffman & Hallahan, 1995, p. 312).

The reaction against the integration of students with significant disabilities into regular schools and classrooms has been so strong that TASH, an advocacy group promoting integration, adopted the slogan "All means all," which reflects the group's efforts to clarify its goal to promote integration for students with significant disabilities.

Another source of criticism has come from within the disability community (Kauffman & Hallahan, 1995).[1] Deaf advocates have expressed concerns over the lack of language development and communication access many deaf children experience in regular classes (Lane, in Kauffman & Hallahan, 1995). Advocates for the learning disabled, such as respected researchers Douglas and Lynn Fuchs, have questioned the ability of regular education classrooms to provide the intensive help these students need for skill development.

> Many students with learning disabilities, then, have learning needs substantially different in amount and kind from those of non-disabled children. An important implication, we believe, is that full-time placement of all students with learning disabilities in mainstream classrooms will result in the failure of some to obtain an appropriate education or one from which they will benefit. No doubt general education can be made more accommodating to student diversity through important innovations such as cooperative learning, but we believe that there are limits on just how resourceful and responsive the mainstream can become. (Fuchs & Fuchs, 1995, p. 524)

These criticisms receive some support from research. The National Longitudinal Transition Study (NLTS) documented that many students integrated into regular education classrooms did not receive much in the way of accommodation or support and that many who were integrated into regular classes failed, thus increasing their likelihood of dropping out (Wagner et al., 1993).

---

1. The term *community* is used loosely here to include those who have disabilities, parents of children with disabilities, and their advocates.

Further, as the research on learning disabilities discussed in the first chapter documents, many children mainstreamed into regular classes experienced little growth in reading in general education classrooms, while carefully constructed special education interventions resulted in improvement (Torgesen, 2000; Torgesen et al., 2001; Vaughn & Fuchs, 2003).

The issue is so controversial within the community that virtually every disability group has developed a position. For example, TASH's strong support for full inclusion is evident in its "Resolution on the Retention of the Continuum of Services":

> TASH further believes that effective methodologies and models which can be applied in integrated settings now exist, and that the focus of new significant and systematic research and development efforts should now be upon development, implementation, validation, and dissemination of such alternatives to outdated practices which segregate persons with disabilities from their families, peers, and community by requiring placement in handicapped-only and categorically grouped services and settings. (Kauffman & Hallahan, 1995, p. 317)

This position is contrasted with that of the Learning Disabilities Association of America:

> The Learning Disabilities Association of America does not support "full inclusion" or practices that mandate the same placement for all students with disabilities. Many students with disabilities benefit from being served in the regular classroom. However, the regular classroom is not the appropriate placement for a number of students with learning disabilities who may need alternative instructional environments, teaching strategies and/or materials that cannot or will not be provided within the context of a regular classroom. (Kauffman & Hallahan, 1995, p. 340)

The controversy over inclusion within the disability community is ultimately dysfunctional and allows those who would limit the rights of students with disabilities to use this as a wedge issue. Fortunately, the community united during the reauthorization of the IDEA in 1997 and again in 2004 to help prevent a weakening of the act. However, threats to the IDEA's fundamental protections remain. The 2004 House bill would have enabled schools to fully exclude some students with disabilities. Fortunately, the Senate bill restored these rights, and the final law that emerged from Congress continued to prohibit cessation of services. In order to fight potential regressive provisions in the future, the community must be united. (A comprehensive discussion of current policy issues is the subject of chapter 6.)

I believe the lens of ableism provides a useful perspective through which the inclusion issue can be resolved within the disability community. First, there needs to be a recognition that education plays a central role in the integration of disabled people in all aspects of society both by giving children the education they need to compete and by demonstrating to nondisabled children that disability is a natural aspect of life. Central to this role is the need for students with disabilities to have access to the same curriculum provided to nondisabled children. Further, education plays a vital role in building communities in which disabled children should be included. Therefore, for most children with disabilities, integration into regular classes with appropriate accommodations and support should be the norm.

## JUSTIFICATIONS FOR REMOVAL

However, the lens of ableism and the goal of minimizing the impact of disability should lead to the recognition that for some students there are strong justifications for some educational services outside the general education classroom. First, there are certain disability-related skills that might need attention outside the regular classroom. Learning Braille or ASL or how to use a communication device are typically not included in the curriculum and might be more efficiently taught outside the mainstream classroom. Further, providing this instruction in a general education classroom may bring unwanted attention to the disabled child. However, caution is called for here as well. Again, Adrienne Asch's experience is relevant here:

> Yet, reflecting on why public school worked for me, I can vouch for the ways professionals either helped or hindered. First my parents were not alone in our belief that I belonged in public school. The New Jersey commission for the Blind aided them in calming anxious administrators before I began public school and sometimes intervened with skeptical teachers during my years there. And, unlike students caught in cynical versions of mainstreaming, I was not dumped without services: my Braille or recorded books were generally on schedule (except for the times when we started a unit at the back of the book that would not be ready until Spring); a teacher knowledgeable in Braille and various other specifics usually checked in with me at the school once a week to help keep things running smoothly. My parents had people they could call if they thought I was missing out on things or having problems related to my blindness or to people's attitude about my blindness. Best of all from my standpoint, the contact with the "Commission" was minimal, intruding relatively little on my school day, rarely taking me out of class for more than two hours a week. More contact and more special help would have heightened my sense of differentness when what I wanted was to be a member of the fourth-grade class and fit in. The experience of overzealous specialists, often mentioned by parents was rare for me. (Ferguson & Asch, 1989, p. 125)

Also, it is important to recognize the importance of students using these disability-specific skills in real-world settings. Therefore, the argument that disabled students may need to be fully segregated in order to learn these skills should be greeted with a degree of skepticism. For instance, a child who has learned to use a communication device needs to feel comfortable using it to communicate with his nondisabled peers if the ultimate goal is for him to live in an integrated society. Most deaf children who go on to higher education will do so in mainstream universities (Postsecondary Education Programs, 2005); they certainly should have educational experiences within the hearing world prior to higher education enrollment. Therefore, fully segregating disabled students for their entire K–12 education is a highly questionable practice that is unlikely to support societal integration.

Another justification for providing educational services outside of the classroom is the provision of intensive intervention in areas where the child is significantly behind his age-level peers or when the regular class cannot reasonably provide the optimal conditions for learning. The example that comes to mind is the need for many dyslexic students to have intensive help in reading through much of their school careers. To reiterate the discussion in the first chapter, research in dyslexia shows clearly that these children can learn to read, but they most likely will need more time and intensive help to do so. Creating the conditions in general education classrooms, particularly beyond the primary grades, for this intensive instruction to occur is difficult and may be undesirable.

My own experience as a high school special education teacher in the 1970s bears this out. I was responsible for a group of seven severely dyslexic students who were reading below the third-grade level. I could have integrated them into English classes with accommodations, and I had considered that option. However, I felt, and they readily agreed, that it was more important at this time for them to learn to read and write. Though reading and writing were very difficult for them, they all were highly motivated and made solid gains over two years, most reaching a fifth-grade level. Though some might consider this a modest gain, they did reach a level of basic literacy and with the strategies they had learned were able to handle materials above that level. I did not believe then, nor do I believe now, that the conditions necessary for these students to learn how to read could have been created in a general education English class. However, removal from other classes was not justified because, given accommodations, they were able to access curriculum I was not qualified to teach. This was particularly the case because I taught in a vocational high school. Special education teachers teaching subjects they are not qualified to teach is a common practice that likely increases the impact of disability. All but one of these students graduated and went on to successful careers in the trades. I believe their success was due to both the availability of specialized intensive help as well as the educational opportunities they could only experience in an integrated environment.

Another reason that students may need to receive services outside the general education class is the need to learn skills within community settings. It is important to note that this may be an important facet of education for both disabled and nondisabled students. All students in the vocational school in which I taught had placements in real jobs within the community before they graduated, so it is possible to structure integrated opportunities to meet this need (Jorgensen, 1997). However, some students with disabilities, particularly those with mental retardation, may need a considerable amount of community-based instruction if they are going to be successful as adults. The nature of mental retardation is such that these children typically have difficulty generalizing and therefore must practice skills in the environment in which they will be used (Brown et al., 1991). Therefore, as children move to adulthood, teaching vocational and independent livings skills within the community is essential. It is, however, important not to take this too far and deny these young people more typical high school experiences and the learning opportunities that can only take place in high school. In my opinion, schools emphasize functional and community skills too much and too early with children with mental retardation. Further, many families are actively involved in teaching these children these skills during nonschool time.

Having a typical high school experience is important for children with cognitive disabilities. Social relationships important in later life are often formed in high school. Further, it is important for these children to also address the developmental issues that high school students experience. Susan Shapiro-Barnard writes:

> Think about your own high school experience for a moment. What are the most important skills you learned? What lessons helped you become a successful adult? Perhaps you learned to manage

time, organize materials, or work with other people. Perhaps you learned to read, communicate ideas, or locate resources for information. Or perhaps you learned to keep going when the going got tough, to read people "between the lines" or to defend your beliefs. Most likely your ability to convert moles to grams and your skills with a food processor are not the basis of your success. (Quoted in Jorgensen, 1997, p. 4)

It is important to instill a love of learning in all children, including those with disabilities. A young woman with Down's syndrome has spoken to my class eloquently about how she related to the disability themes in the novel *Stones from the River,* which she read in her English class. This young woman also spoke enthusiastically about her experience in the drama club and her role in school plays. Another boy with disabilities, the son of a friend, recounted to me how he had learned about slave and free states in his social studies class and how that was important to him as an African American. These are important lessons that are not taught in functional curricula, and they underscore the importance of access to the curriculum for all students. Assuming that the entire education of any child with a disability be "functional" is unduly limiting, deadly boring, and at its root ableist.

The choice between community-based instruction and more typical high school experiences for students with mental retardation is largely an unnecessary one. Special education eligibility in most states extends to age 21 or 22. Therefore, there is time for both. Students may have a typical high school experience for four years while engaging in a robust transition program from ages 18 to 22, during which time they refine their vocational and independent living skills. Some community colleges have responded with programs tailored to the needs of young adults with cognitive disabilities transitioning to adulthood.

The discussion of inclusive education would be incomplete without returning to the issue of the inappropriate use of paraprofessionals. As discussed in the first chapter, the inappropriate use of paraprofessionals may reflect ableist assumptions about children with disabilities and can have negative consequences for children. Their use may reflect the assumption that children with disabilities cannot do things on their own and may inordinately emphasize difference.

The potential overuse of paraprofessionals was brought home to me recently during a meeting of parents of children with disabilities in a suburban Boston community. The group was small, so before I began my presentation I asked them to describe their children to me. Each began by identifying his or her child's disability, and a common ending was, "He's fully included and has a full-time para." After I had heard four parents in a row repeat this mantra, I asked if they thought that having a "full-time para" was a good thing. They looked at me a bit confused. I told them that I thought their desire for inclusion and the district's willingness to provide it was positive, but I challenged them to examine whether the provision of a full-time paraprofessional might have some negative unintended consequences. A rich discussion ensued in which the parents discussed their hopes for their children, their desire for them to live in an integrated community with friends, and their belief in their children's potential. However, it appeared that they had not really considered the potential pitfalls of full-time paraprofessionals. These parents were experiencing an increasingly common pattern of inclusive education implementation, the assignment of paraprofessionals in response to the increasing pressure of parents who want inclusive education for their children (Giangreco et al., 1997).

These parents as well as educators could benefit significantly from the research of Giangreco and his colleagues. Their study, "Helping or Hovering? The Effects of Instructional Assistant Proximity on Students with Disabilities," is a well-constructed qualitative study of 11 students with multiple disabilities educated in inclusive settings in four states. It documents the unintended consequences of this practice. Though their study size is small, and, therefore, caution must be taken in generalizing its results, their findings are consistent with the observations of many of my students who work in over 20 schools in the Boston area. Further, the study and the authors' recommendations provide solid guidance to parents and educators implementing inclusive education.

The disturbing findings in their study seem to stem from the close proximity between the assistants in their study and the students they serve. Though some of this proximity may have been necessary, the authors also observed unnecessary and excessive adult proximity. The analysis of their data revealed eight subthemes pertaining to proximity that raise serious concern.

One potentially negative impact of proximity identified in their study is the interference with ownership and responsibility on the part of general educators. They found that "although special educators and related services providers were involved in each case, almost universally it was the instructional assistants who were given the responsibility and ownership for educating students with disabilities." This is a frequent observation of my students as well. The seriousness of this finding is compounded by the fact that most of the assistants were woefully unprepared for this role, with most receiving only on-the-job training. This lack of training can result in incompetent instruction.

Though one of the most frequently cited reasons by parents for inclusion of their significantly disabled children is the desire for them to develop social relationships with their peers, this study found that the excessive proximity of teacher assistants may inhibit this goal. Classroom assistants were regularly observed separating students with disabilities from classroom groupings and at times interfered with peer interactions. One special educator in the study observed, "Sometimes I think it inhibits her relationship with her peers because a lot is done for Holly and Holly doesn't have the opportunity to interact with her peers because there is always somebody hovering over her showing her what to do or doing things for her. I'd like to get the instructional assistant away from Holly a little bit more so that peers will have a chance to get in there and work more with Holly" (Giangreco et al., 1997, p. 13). Other negative consequences found in this study included loss of personal control by the students, who were not encouraged to express their own desires or preferences, and a loss of gender identity.

Giangreco and his colleagues go on to discuss the practical implications of their study. Though they acknowledge that instructional assistants have an important role in inclusive education, they recommend, among other things, that districts rethink their policies, including hiring assistants for classrooms as opposed to individual students, that schools and families reach an agreement on when students need close proximity, that roles be clarified, and that improved training of paraprofessionals occur.

## IMPORTANT CONSIDERATIONS RELEVANT TO INCLUSION DECISIONS

### 1. General education environments should be the presumed placement for all students with disabilities.

The IDEA has sought the integration of students with disabilities from its inception with its least restrictive environment (LRE) provisions. These regulations state that "special education class, separate schooling and other removal of children with disabilities from regular education environment occurs only if the nature and severity of the disability is such that education in regular class with the use of supplementary aids and services cannot be achieved" (IDEA 1997, 300.550). This is a strong standard that in effect puts the burden on school districts to justify removal. Basically, the courts have provided consistent support to parents who have sought sensible inclusion in general classes (Hehir & Gamm, 1999). More recently, the Supreme Court, in *Garett Fry v. Cedar Rapids*, found that the district's attempts to remove a young boy with spinal chord injury from regular education to home school instruction violated the IDEA even though his medical supports were costly.

It should also be noted that LRE is a dynamic standard that changes as new methodologies and technologies develop over time. The courts have recognized this as well. In the Oberti decision (*Oberti v. Board of Education*, 1993) the court relied heavily on expert testimony to reach its decision in favor of the inclusion of Rafael, a student with Down's syndrome who had significant learning and behavior issues. Essentially, the plaintiffs in the case demonstrated that similar children had been successfully included in other districts by employing innovative strategies. The burden therefore fell on the school district to justify its proposed segregated placement: "The court discounted the district's expert testimony that the regular teacher would not be able to communicate with Rafael and the curriculum would be modified beyond recognition to accommodate him. Instead the court was persuaded by parents' experts, who pointed to various 'commonly applied methods' that could be used by the teacher, with appropriate training" (Hehir & Gamm, 1999, p. 221). Educators and parents need to be cognizant of new developments in the field that will likely continue to demonstrate how students can be successfully supported in general education.

It is important to reiterate here that the strong legal support for integration also comports well with the preponderance of research. Integration in regular education classes is associated with better outcomes such as employment, postsecondary education, and income (Wagner et al., 1993). Further, the reverse hypothesis that full segregation is superior for any group of disabled students has very little support and much evidence to the contrary. These findings may reflect simple common sense. It is simply very difficult to prepare children for the real world in an artificial environment.

Finally, if we are going to eliminate ableism in our society, nondisabled children need to have positive experiences with children with disabilities. As children are educated together they will develop friendships, and disability will cease to be surrounded by fear and myth. The children of today will be the parents of the next generation of children with disabilities.

## 2. Removal should only occur if important learning goals cannot be achieved in the general education environment.

Though there is relatively strong support for inclusion in the research, many of the studies compare totally segregated populations with integrated ones. However, the research does not support the proposition that all children with disabilities should be educated all the time in general education classrooms (Hocutt, 1996; Torgesen, 2000; Torgesen et al., 2001). To reiterate, the population of children with disabilities is large and diverse. A successful practice for one group may not be appropriate for another. There are justifiable reasons for removal, as discussed earlier in this chapter. The law supports this as well with its requirement for a continuum of services (IDEA 1997, 300.553).

### 3. Removal should not occur simply because general education refuses to accommodate the needs of children with disabilities.

As a special education teacher I practiced the high art of negotiation in order to integrate "my kids" into general education classrooms. Some teachers were a godsend for the students I served, while others I avoided totally. Looking back, I have mixed feelings about this behavior. On the one hand, I was successful in attaining important educational experiences for students with disabilities. On the other hand, I believe I was cooperating with a practice of discrimination that is illegal and immoral. However, this was the seventies, and for that time these were progressive practices. I am dismayed, however, about feedback I get from special educators and parents indicating that this practice of negotiation and avoidance continues in many American schools.

Students with disabilities have the right to the accommodations, modifications, and supports they need to be successful in general education classrooms, and no teacher or administrator should be allowed to abridge that right. The law is clear on that. Yet I hear anecdotes from parents and teachers frequently that children are not allowed in general education classes because they cannot read on grade level, or because they need support in meeting classroom behavioral requirements, or because they are not functioning on grade level. The "tolerance" level for this discriminatory behavior, in my view, is way too high and is a reflection of ableism. Fortunately, we are at a point in this country where exclusion based on race or gender would be met with swift governmental action and headlines in most local papers. The same should be the case with inappropriate disability exclusion. The fact that it is not is a reflection of deeply rooted ableism within schools and the broader society.

Though it may be difficult for advocates, parents, and school personnel to force integration upon a recalcitrant teacher or administrator, we must do so. Failure to do so will keep the system in place and result in lost opportunities for students. What if the recalcitrant teacher is the only one teaching advanced mathematics? What if a child with a disability has moved through the first three grades successfully with his friends and then encounters a fourth-grade teacher who erects barriers to his participation? From its inception, the IDEA has been about changing how schools serve students with disabilities. Difficult as it may be, we must continue to push for full access for all students and hold school officials accountable for that result.

### 4. Social integration is important.

In a presentation on inclusion to a group of superintendents I was once asked, rather incredulously, whether I felt it was appropriate for schools to help children make friends. I answered that I did and that the role of schools in building community has long been recognized. Fostering good citizenship is an important role of schools, and the development of positive social relationships among students is an obvious means toward that end. As the narratives in Biklen make clear, many parents of children with significant cognitive disabilities deeply value the establishment of friendships. The role of schools in fostering integration may take on even more importance for schools given that friendships for many of these students may not happen as naturally as they do for other children. To help achieve this goal innovative educators have developed programs like Circle of Friends that provide systematic approaches for the development of social relationships between significantly disabled students and nondisabled students.

There are other important reasons, beyond the obvious joys of friendship, why the development of social relationships is important. An important one is that students with significant disabilities need to begin to develop supports within their community that can help them stay in the community long after they leave school. Many hope that childhood relationships will help serve this purpose. Also, the development of positive social relationships through membership in organized activities is correlated with overall outcomes for students with milder disabilities (Wagner et al., 1993).

It is important to note here that many people with disabilities also consider the development of social relationships with other children with disabilities as very important. Judy Heumann recalls the profound influence her attendance at a camp for disabled students had on her development as an activist. In recalling this camp experience, Judy credited this time as an important part of her formation as an activist: "We danced and we danced so well we felt good about ourselves." She went on to discuss how they dated and "talked about getting married, where you couldn't talk about that at home" (quoted in Shapiro, 1994, p. 103). Adrienne Asch reports a similar experience (Ferguson & Asch, 1989).

It is a bit disconcerting that some advocates of inclusion do not seem to understand the importance of disabled children developing friendships with other disabled students. It appears that the only social relationships valued are those with nondisabled or "typical" children. This is unfortunate, and it reminds me of a question that was asked of me by the parent of a child with Down's syndrome at a workshop I was conducting on inclusion. She told me that her daughter was "fully included" in her neighborhood suburban school. When this mother asked her daughter what she wanted to do on Saturday, her daughter would reply that she wanted to play with another girl with Down's syndrome she had met at church. The girl's mother asked me if she should "let her," fearing that the other child was not a "typical role model." I responded that of course she should honor her daughter's request and that her daughter's ability to express a preference was a sign in my mind of maturity and autonomy, both desirable outcomes. This mother was noticeably relieved at my response. She was obviously struggling mightily to do the best for her daughter and appeared to be succeeding. The advocacy for "nondisabled-only" friendship development in my view may reflect ableism at its core in that it implies a devaluing of disability. Had this mother refused to allow her daughter to visit her friend, she might have inadvertently communicated a negative message to her daughter about her disability. Most would consider it strange if a Jewish parent did not want her children to associate with other Jewish kids. We should view the desire of disabled students to make friendships with other disabled students in the same light and indeed provide opportunities for these relationships to develop.

### 5. *Inclusion should be purposeful.*

In some discussions I have had with advocates and parents I have gotten the impression that "full inclusion" is the goal, not the means to an end. In my mind we should never lose sight of the goal of high-quality education for all students, for which inclusion is a necessary means toward that end. During a discussion I had in class one day after my students had read Biklen's book, I asked my students, most of whom were experienced general educators, whether they would accept one of the students described in the book in their classroom. A high school math teacher responded, "I would like to know why the student was placed there. What would the expectations of me be?" He went on to say that he would consider it totally appropriate for the students with mental retardation to be in his class if the goals were clear and if he received support.

As should be clear thus far, simply placing students with disabilities in general education does not guarantee good results. Further, there are sound justifications for some removal. The decision to integrate a child should be a deliberate one in which team members and parents are clear about the instructional goals. For most children with disabilities the goals should be those contained within the curriculum with appropriate accommodations and support. However, some students, particularly those with mental retardation, may need modified curriculum. The IDEA provides for this by prohibiting removal due solely to need to modify curriculum (IDEA 1997, 300.552). Some children, particularly those with more significant disabilities, may have goals relating to behavior, social, or language development for which inclusive environments provide the greatest opportunities for growth. The point is that goals should be clear to all concerned. The research by Giangreco and colleagues leads me to conclude that the instructional goals for these students were very unclear. (A more detailed discussion of issues surrounding accommodations and modifications appears in chapter 4.)

In order to prevent the rather aimless situations described by Giangreco and colleagues, educators and parents making integration decisions for students with mental retardation should be guided by the research on learning for these students. Brown and colleagues (1991) in their seminal piece "How Much Time Should Students with Severe Intellectual Disabilities Spend in Regular Education Classrooms and Elsewhere?" summarized the salient findings from research regarding learning for students with mental retardation. These principles include the fact that students with significant intellectual disabilities can learn relatively few skills at a time, tend to be concrete as opposed to abstract learners, require more instructional trials to acquire skills, are more prone to forgetting, and tend to have great difficulty generalizing. Based on these findings, Brown and his colleagues went on to suggest factors to be considered when making decisions on whether to integrate students within general education classrooms. These include (1) acknowledging the importance of taking into account the chronological age of the child with the recognition that as the child grows older, he or she may need to spend more time in community and work settings; (2) being sensitive to the fact that some related services such as speech therapy and occupational therapy may be more appropriately provided in natural environments such as general education classes or job sites, while other services may require a degree of privacy that makes their provision in general education classrooms inappropriate; (3) recognizing that the development of a student's ability to demonstrate skills in different environments may necessitate time spent in a variety of environments; and (4) granting the importance of contact with general education students as a means to develop social relationships (Brown et al., 1991, pp. 116, 117).

If we use these principles when we make decisions concerning the integration of students with mental retardation, we will increase the likelihood that they will learn. The expectation that these children will learn to their optimal level because they are in environments with nondisabled students is not supported by research. Therefore, the integration of these students should be purposeful and structured to produce optimal learning.

Further, there may be times when educators and parents might decide that the general education class is not the optimal setting in which to learn a specific skill. An example of this might be reading instruction. Most children with mental retardation can and should learn to read. In order to achieve this goal the student may have to be pulled out for intensive help. However, once the child has approached his or her reading expectancy level, integration into regular classes with accommodations or modifications may be equally important. That environment allows children to practice their skills broadly and may encourage a lifelong love of reading, as was the case with the girl reading *Stones from the River*.

It should also be emphasized that applying what is known about learning to students with mental retardation also leads us to question the total segregation of these students. Segregated classes are very unnatural environments, and generalization cannot occur within them. Therefore, integration of these students into more natural environments is clearly indicated. The point here is that full inclusion all the time may not result in the optimal learning outcomes for these students. Further, integration that is not well planned out with clear learning goals runs the risk of wasting valuable instructional time for these students. Assuming it is accept-able to simply place students with disabilities in general education classes without providing real learning opportunities may rein-force ableism by inadvertently communicating the message that these children cannot learn or that they need full-time assistance in order to make it in the world. Further, as is the case with all chil-dren, if these children leave school undereducated, their life op-tions will be greatly restricted.

The debate over inclusion is a completely unnecessary one. The acceptance of the goals of minimizing the impact of disabil-ity while maximizing opportunities to participate provides a use-ful framework that can lead to sensible decisions for children with disabilities. We should be united around the importance of soci-etal integration while recognizing that the difference inherent in disability is a positive one that at times gives rise to individual or disability-specific educational needs. This framework helps advo-cates move away from the fight over placement to one that focus-es on educational results. The next chapter focuses on the promise of universal design. Universally designed schools and programs that consider the needs of disabled students from their inception can greatly increase opportunities for the integration of children with disabilities while minimizing the impact of their disabilities.

# Toward Ending Ableism in Education

## The Promise of Universal Design

> I'm not seeking anything "special." I just want access to the library. And in an age of high speed scanners, I can't for the life of me figure out why it's difficult to get digitized text.
>
> —*Joe Ford, Harvard College, Class of 2006*

An issue that logically arises out of the inclusion discussion is the promise of universal design. Simply put, the schools that have taken into account the needs of disabled children in their design are better able to effectively educate these students without having to resort to special means. Essentially, the concept of universal design originated in architecture through the work of Ron Mace, who seeks to design and construct buildings to accommodate the widest spectrum of users without the need for subsequent adaptation and retrofitting (Rose & Meyer, 2002). This concept has been expanded to other spheres of life in which disabled people seek access, from technology to the classroom.

Joe Ford, quoted above, requires digitized text, which he can access through software on his computer, which can then "read" the text to him. Texts in the library could be scanned and sent to him through email attachments. This is mainstream technology. However, Harvard refused to do this, even though the library has several high-speed scanners and many work-study students who could easily do the scanning. The university requires students to obtain a photocopy of the document and bring it to a "special" technology center in another building, where the material is scanned on an old, low-speed scanner when someone gets around to it. Joe has waited as long as two weeks to get material he needs to do his research. How can he be expected to do research this way? Further, how much time and money is the university wasting on an outmoded "special" technology center? (This situation has improved; see Epilogue.)

This situation would be easily resolved if the university recognized the promise of universal design. As technology advances and we develop new instructional approaches, there will be increasing options for disabled students to gain access to opportunities that may have been closed to them or only available to them through extraordinary means.

However, as is the case with racism and sexism, progress toward equity is dependent first and foremost on the acknowledgment that ableism exists in schools. Harvard prides itself on its diversity efforts, with significant resources devoted to preventing racism, sexism, and homophobia. However, disability is not often part of the diversity discussion.

The lack of attention to this issue at the university may be due to the absence of discussion and the dearth of scholarly inquiry within mainstream education circles concerning the effects of ableism. Though the lack of attention to ableism in schooling is unfortunate, activists within the disability community have long recognized its impact (Rauscher & McClintock, 1996). Therefore, as more adults with disabilities take on more powerful roles in society and seek to influence schooling (as I am sure this student will), the attention to these issues will increase (Shapiro, 1994). In addition to this political force, the lack of acceptable educational outcomes for large numbers of children with disabilities in an era of standards-based reform should force a reexamination of current practices. Universal design holds much promise here. (Chapter 5 addresses the importance of standards-based reforms in improving educational outcomes for students with disabilities.)

First and foremost, it is important to include disability as part of schools' overall diversity efforts. Schools are increasingly recognizing the need to explicitly address diversity issues as the country becomes more racially and ethnically diverse. Some schools are expanding diversity efforts to include disability. Recently, a local high school student with Down's syndrome whom I had met at a school assembly devoted to issues of disability rights addressed one of my classes. She stated, "There are all kinds of kids at my school: black kids, Puerto Rican kids, gay and lesbian kids. Meagan uses a wheelchair, Matt's deaf, and I have Down's syndrome. It's all diversity." Her high school has done a great job of including disabled students and has incorporated discussions about disability in its efforts to address diversity issues. Adults with disabilities address student groups, and disability is presented in a natural way. Students learn about people with disabilities who have achieved great things as well as those who live ordinary lives. People with disabilities are not presented in a patronizing or stereotypical manner. Deaf people are not "hearing challenged," and people with mental retardation are not "very special." Ableism is not the norm; disability is dealt with in a straightforward manner. In schools like this, students with disabilities learn about their disabilities and learn how to be self-advocates (Jorgensen, 1997).

This recognition of disability as a basic diversity issue, that disability is not to be pitied, patronized, or vilified, is important if disabled students are going to feel comfortable being disabled. Students with disabilities are unlikely to progress as well in school and in life if they are ashamed of their disability or uncomfortable disclosing it. Without this comfort students may be incapacitated in dealing with the "difference" issues that arise out of their disability such as their needs for accommodation and support. Therefore, the need to provide a supportive environment in which disabled students can learn is directly tied to improving educational results.

Dealing with diversity issues alone is not sufficient to improve educational prospects for disabled students. Improved educational practices are also needed. Fortunately, as should be clear, there is a foundation in both research and practice upon which to build a better future. Promising research is demonstrating how schools can be more successful with all students with disabilities. A particularly important line of thinking and research has involved bringing the concept of universal design to schooling. As previously stated, this concept, which was first applied to architecture, calls for the design of buildings with the assumption that people with disabilities would be using them. With the legal backing of the Americans with Disabilities Act, these principles are applied increasingly to new construction and renovation of public buildings. Ramps, automatic door-opening devices, accessible toilets, and fire alarm systems with lights activated for the deaf are examples of universal design features incorporated into contemporary buildings. Other examples extend to technologies. Captioning devices are required features on all televisions, and digital text can be read from computers with screen readers. Universal design allows for access without extraordinary means and is based on the assumption that disabled people are numerous and should be able to lead regular lives.

However, the concept of universal design has yet to become widespread in schooling. For instance, as the discussion in the previous chapter on early reading demonstrates, even though learning disabilities are common in students, we have yet to design our reading programs with these children in mind (Lyon et al., 2001). We tend to have "one size fits all" reading programs in the primary grades. This is true of other areas as well, such as how schools handle students with disabilities that affect behavior. Using the analogy of architecture, we often attempt to retrofit the children with inappropriate interventions after they have failed in school rather than design the instructional program from the beginning to allow for access and success. And, as is the case with architecture, the failure to design universally is inefficient and ineffective.

Support for the concept of universal design comes from a long line of theory and research that posits that disability is heavily socially constructed, that disability is largely determined by the demands of society and the way in which society responds to difference. The work of Nora Groce (1985) concerning the deaf people on Martha's Vineyard referred to in chapter 1 is a frequently cited example of this frame for viewing disability. The fact that most residents on the Vineyard in the 1880s could sign meant that deafness had relatively little impact on the deaf residents of the island. Deborah Stone's (1984) work on income support programs for people with disabilities deemed unable to work, like the Social Security Disability Income program, is another example of this tradition in disability scholarship.

In the contemporary school context in the United States and other economically developed countries, the extension of the concept of the social construction of disability has clear relevance. For instance, the largest disability category served under the Individuals with Disabilities Education Act (IDEA), learning disability (LD), is almost always associated with marked difficulty in reading, writing, and spelling. Therefore, in a society where literacy demands are minimal, it is likely that this disability would go largely unnoticed.

Disability theorists, advocates, and researchers often engage in lively debates concerning the question of whether disability is socially constructed. Though I have enjoyed these debates with colleagues and friends, as a practical matter I believe that the most important dimension is functionality, not whether disability is intrinsically "caused" or externally defined. Students who cannot read well are functionally disabled in most school settings, and students who cannot meet the behavioral requirements of schools are likely to experience very negative outcomes in school and life (Wagner et al., 1993).

The debate about the origin of disability has played out in profound ways in special education policy and implementation. As the discussion in the previous chapter concerning learning disability determination illustrates, the search for an intrinsic cause in the determination of eligibility has resulted in less than optimal interventions based on assumptions that are largely nonscientific, resulting in educational harm for many students. These esteemed researchers' recognition that learning disabilities can only be determined accurately after interventions is a support for the importance of focusing on functionality as the primary dimension (Lyon et al., 2001). This is not to say that dyslexia does not have an intrinsic element. There are clear neurological and even genetic markers of this disability (Shaywitz, 2003). The point is that dyslexia is highly responsive to context (how reading is taught) and that some students can be functionally disabled due to educational and environmental deprivation. Indeed, the IDEA has incorporated both the medical (intrinsic origin) model and the social construction (social systems) model in the way it determines disability (McDonnell et al., 1997). However, traditional LD definitions incorporated in the regulatory definition of LD are oriented to intrinsic causation (IDEA 1997, Regulations 300.7 (10)).

Many school personnel fear the use of more functional dimensions for determining disability because they fear an explosion of referrals. After all, there are many students doing poorly in school who might be considered functionally disabled. However, as we focus more attention on standards, hopefully fewer and fewer students will be left behind. Further, it is important to acknowledge that our current system of disability determination is hardly objective. The great variability of identification rates from state to state and even within states attests to this (U.S. Department of Education, 2003). And, as the research of Beth Harry and her colleagues (2002) has shown, the way in which school personnel approach disability determination is frequently manipulated and subjective even when "objective" psychological tests are used.

It is also important to recognize that the most relevant functional dimensions in disability determination in school-aged children are reading ability and behavioral adjustment. Most referrals to special education result from concerns in these two areas. Researchers have clearly shown that attention to concepts of universal design in these two areas can actually decrease the number of students who will need special education and allow for a more concentrated attention to those who need the greatest supports.

An interesting by-product of universal design is the benefit it brings to nondisabled people as well. People pushing baby carriages appreciate curb cuts. Hearing people trying to keep up with the Super Bowl in a noisy bar can do so via captioning. The same can be said for education. Reading programs that are successful with dyslexic students will be better able to reach those who may be struggling for other reasons. A school that includes a child with autism or other disabilities that result in behavioral issues is likely to be a school that can serve others with behavior problems more effectively (Sugai et al., 2000). However, I do not believe that disability services should be justified on the basis of their impact on the nondisabled. Universal design is a matter of simple justice. I mention these examples here simply to increase the force of the argument that universal design is truly universal in its impact.

In this chapter I present four areas in which the concept of universal design is emerging in research and has great potential for improving education for students with disabilities as well as other students. The first involves universal design of reading programs. This discussion builds on the previous discussion on treatment-resistant models of disability determination and incorporates other relevant reading research, particularly the research synthesis conducted by the National Research Council (NRC), *Preventing Reading Difficulties in Young Children* (Snow, 1998). The second area concerns the universal design of curriculum developed by Rose and his colleagues that seeks the development of learning approaches that help assure access to learning for diverse learners.

The third area involves the universal design of school behavioral support and discipline programs, drawing heavily on the work of Horner, Sugai, Walker, and their colleagues. The final discussion applies the concept of universal design to school organization and draws on the work of Elmore and Skrtic.

## UNIVERSAL DESIGN AND READING

A majority of students with disabilities are at risk of reading failure. Students with learning disabilities, students with hearing impairments, and students with cognitive disabilities are all likely to experience difficulty learning to read. The very nature of these disabilities frequently produces impediments to learning to read. It should not be inferred that these students cannot learn to read, but significant attention must be paid to needs that arise out of their disabilities.

Students with disabilities are not the only children at risk of reading failure. Poor reading outcomes are also associated with poverty and minority status as well as with many children who are learning English. This association "no doubt reflects the accumulated effects of several risk factors, including lack of access to literacy-stimulating preschool experiences and to excellent, coherent reading instruction" (Snow, 1998, p. 4). Given the centrality of competent reading to all educational attainment, is it possible to design reading programs that prevent reading failure among those at risk, both disabled and nondisabled? The NRC study (Snow, 1998) and the work of Lyon and colleagues (2001) present a comprehensive understanding of reading failure across populations of students and thus provide a useful lens with which to examine the potential of universal design of reading programs.

Before moving into the specifics of universally designed reading programs it is important to summarize some of the more salient insights we have gained about reading failure presented in the NRC report. First, with regard to typical reading development, reading skill is acquired in a relatively predictable way by children who have normal or above average language skills; have had experiences in early childhood that fostered motivation and provided exposure to literacy in use; get information about the nature of print through opportunities to learn letters and recognize the internal structure of spoken words, as well as explanations about the contrasting nature of spoken and written language; attend schools that provide effective instruction and opportunities to practice reading. (Snow, 1998, p. 4)

Of course, some students with disabilities do not have normal intelligence or have hearing or other impairments that may interfere with normal language development. Therefore, these students are likely to need services to address these needs. However, this foundation is a useful one on which to base the discussion of universal design in that it identifies the likely areas where specialized interventions will be necessary.

The report goes on to identify three potential stumbling blocks that can interfere with a child becoming a skilled reader.

The first obstacle, which arises at the onset of reading acquisition, is difficulty understanding and using the alphabetic principle—the idea that written spellings systematically represent spoken words. It is hard to comprehend connected word text if recognition is inaccurate or laborious. The second obstacle is a failure to transfer the comprehension skills of spoken language to reading and acquire new strategies that may be specifically needed for reading. The third obstacle to reading will magnify the first two: the absence or loss of motivation to read or the failure to develop a mature appreciation of the rewards of reading. (Snow, 1998, p. 4)

The comprehensive synthesis of the research on reading failure presented in the NRC report provides the basis for rather far-reaching recommendations for improving services for young children. Many of these are complementary to the principles of universal design.

## Universally Designed Preschool and Kindergarten Options

The NRC report asserts that the process of learning to read is lengthy and typically begins before children enter school. Opportunities to develop the prerequisite language, motivation, and early literacy skills that predispose children to be successful early readers may not be available for many at-risk children. Preschools and other group care settings, particularly those available for poor children, are often impoverished language and literacy environments. Some children's disabilities may interfere with their language development. For instance, deaf children may need to develop manual language in order to develop the prerequisite language ability for literacy. The NRC report thus recommends that improved preschool opportunities be available to children at risk of reading failure. Specifically, the report recommends that these programs be designed broadly to promote cognitive, language, and social development and that specific attention be paid to the skills that are known to predict future achievement. For instance, the report recommends that kindergarten instruction emphasize verbal interaction, enrich children's vocabularies, encourage talk about books, provide practice with sound structures of words, and develop familiarity with basic purposes and mechanisms of reading (Snow, 1998).

The IDEA has recognized the importance of starting students on the right track early with its early intervention and preschool requirements. It is important that these programs also recognize the specific needs of these children that arise out of their disability and that these programs be based on our best understanding of reading and literacy acquisition. The NRC report states: "Children who are having difficulty learning to read do not, as a rule, require qualitatively different instruction from children who are 'getting it.' Instead they often need application of the same principles by someone who can apply them expertly to individual children who are having difficulty for one reason or the other" (Snow, 1998, p. 12). The report thus recommends that special education personnel base their interventions on the research on reading development and the prevention of reading difficulties.

An important point to emphasize in discussing preschool options for students with disabilities is the fact that most students
with disabilities are not identified prior to entering school. Therefore, most never experience the benefits of these programs. Many,
however, may be within other risk groups that predispose them
to reading difficulties. Students with disabilities are more likely to
come from high poverty backgrounds (Wagner et al., 1993). Thus
the call within the NRC report for greater access to high-quality
preschool options for students from other at-risk groups will benefit students with disabilities and may prevent the need for special
education services later.

Another potentially beneficial aspect to increasing the availability of high-quality preschool programs is the opportunities for
integration these programs could provide to students who have
disabilities. Many special education preschool providers struggle
with providing their students with opportunities to interact with
nondisabled children. This is important not only because the least
restrictive environment provisions of the IDEA apply to preschool
but also because, as the NRC report emphasizes, language development is central to reading. Unfortunately, many disabled students remain in environments in which typically developing language models are not present. Therefore, these students may be
missing important developmental opportunities that are critical to
later success.

The call for greater access to high-quality preschool options for
all students identified as at risk for reading difficulties is a natural opportunity to promote universally designed preschools. First,
there already exists a significant network of special education preschool programs that can serve as building blocks for expanded
access. Second, students with disabilities will benefit from both
the integrative opportunities these programs provide as well as
the fact that these programs incorporate findings from reading research. Finally, students who are not identified could benefit by
having support services on-site that may be potentially beneficial,
such as speech therapists and special educators who may be able

to provide students with important intervention or identify disabilities earlier.

## Universally Designed Early Reading Programs and Disability Identification

As the discussion of treatment-resistant models of disability identification in chapter 1 indicates, the very identification of students with learning disabilities may only be optimally accomplished after research-based interventions in the primary grades. That is, without universally available early intervention for all students experiencing early reading failure, students with learning disabilities will continue to suffer from "wait and fail" approaches, and accurate identification of dyslexia may not be possible. Further, the lack of early interventions may result in functional reading disability in students who otherwise might have been able to become proficient readers. (This issue is discussed in greater depth in chapter 6, which concerns policy.)

The NRC report identifies a number of conditions that schools with large numbers of at-risk students will have to address in order to prevent reading difficulties. Among these are schoolwide restructuring, improved teacher-training efforts, and making available intensive interventions for those most at risk. Though improved preschool options may alleviate the demands on elementary schools to exert extraordinary efforts to prevent reading difficulties, in schools in which large numbers are struggling early reading options will have to be significantly improved. More intensive work will be required of those at greatest risk for early reading failure, including students with disabilities. Many may still not reach grade-level achievement goals.

One common way in which school districts deal with the issue of students failing to meet grade-level standards is to retain students in grade. The NRC report states that this practice lacks a solid research foundation, and another NRC report, *High Stakes: Testing for Tracking, Promotion and Graduation* (Heubert & Hauser, 1999), comes out fairly strongly against the practice. Yet the practice persists. Given the fact that many students with disabilities as well as others who experience early reading difficulty may simply need more time engaged in high-quality instruction, a provision of special education that requires eligible students to receive extended school-year (ESY) services may be another example of how universal design principles can be applied to the area of reading. This option may be clearly preferable to retention. Though ESY services are more commonly utilized with students who have significant disabilities (based on the premise that these services are required because these students experience significant regression and have difficulty recouping skills after the summer break), the same logic could apply to students who are not progressing satisfactorily in reading. Clearly, in the current environment of standards-based reform, not learning to read satisfactorily is a very serious event that warrants extraordinary responses. Therefore, schools should consider extending ESY services both to students with less severe disabilities as well as to other students who are struggling to read. Actually, if we take universal design to its next logical step, we might question the benefit of long summer breaks from school for many students.

Many students who have disabilities such as dyslexia are likely to continue to need support and accommodations throughout their schooling even with the best of services (Shaywitz, 2003). If they are provided with these services, they can have a successful and literate future. In today's digitized age, these accommodations are readily available through promising new instructional technologies that allow for much greater access. These technologies may also be beneficial for others experiencing reading difficulties. A brief discussion of universal design for learning follows.

## UNIVERSAL DESIGN FOR LEARNING

As previously developed, the 1997 amendments to the IDEA emphasize access to the curriculum for all students with disabilities as a means to combat low expectations and improve the life prospects of children with disabilities, thus minimizing the impact of their disabilities. Though this is a strong policy direction, the diverse needs of students with disabilities make implementation in the classroom a significant challenge. Fortunately, innovative researchers began laying a foundation upon which access to the curriculum could be based long before 1997. One particularly promising approach, universal design for learning (UDL), was developed by David Rose and Anne Meyer (2002). This work unites the recent insights derived from brain research with the opportunities provided by the digital age.

Rose and Meyer derive two central principles from brain research. First, "learning is distributed across three interconnected networks: the recognition networks are specialized to receive and analyze information (the 'what' of learning); the strategic networks are specialized to plan and execute actions (the 'how' of learning); and the affective networks are specialized to evaluate and set priorities (the 'why' of learning)" (Rose & Meyer, 2002, p. 11). Second, "learners cannot be reduced to simple categories such as 'disabled' or 'bright.' They differ within and across networks, showing shades of strength and weakness that make them each unique" (Rose & Meyer, 2002, p. 11). These understandings have been greatly influenced by remarkable new technologies such as PET scans that enable researchers to view the working brain.

The advances in technology brought about by the digital age have enabled Rose and Meyer to develop new multimedia approaches that can help remove barriers inherent in traditional teaching methods and curriculum materials. Originally, they worked at developing individually tailored devices that would enable students with disabilities to increase their access to print-based curriculum. These efforts largely provided assistive technology to students with disabilities. However, over time Rose and Meyer evolved into a new role, "the use of technology to transform the nature of the curriculum itself" (2002, p. v). One of their early products, WiggleWorks, codeveloped with Scholastic, Inc., demonstrated that an electronic book could include features that enable all kinds of students to access the material. For instance, students with physical disabilities can turn pages and access controls with the touch of a key or a switch. Students with visual disabilities can expand the size of the print. Students with learning disabilities can have words they are having difficulty decoding read to them. Various "scaffolds" can be individually built into the program that call students' attention to important details or concepts (Rose & Meyer, 2002).

Combining these technologies with neuroscience, Rose and Meyer have developed UDL based on the following principles:

- To support recognition learning, provide multiple, flexible methods of presentation.
- To support strategic learning, provide flexible methods of expression and apprenticeship.
- To support affective learning, provide multiple, flexible options for engagement. (2002, p. 75)

UDL is a giant step away from the classic retrofitting model of education experienced by many students with disabilities. Students do not have to wait for materials to be put on tape or settle for low-level text because they have inadequate decoding skills. All students can deal with the same text tailored to their needs. As in the case with architecture, UDL has demonstrated that it is much more desirable and efficient to design our curricula assuming the participation of the disabled. Such design allows for full participation and access for students with disabilities while providing individualized options for all. More information concerning UDL is available through the National Consortium on UDL (www.cast.org/nationalconsortium).

## UNIVERSALLY DESIGNED SUPPORT FOR POSITIVE BEHAVIOR

Students identified as significantly emotionally disturbed (SED) have experienced the worst outcomes of any population served under the IDEA. Their dropout rates are in the 40 percent range, almost double that of other disability groups (Wagner & Cameto, 2004). As already mentioned in chapter 1, these students have high rates of segregation. Students with this disability have high rates of incarceration, low rates of employment, and low higher education rates after leaving school (Wagner & Cameto, 2004; Wagner et al., 1991).

It is clear that we are failing these children in large numbers. One reason for these dismal results may be the relatively high rates of segregation these students experience, as there is a correlation between levels of segregation and postschool outcomes. However, I believe the basis of their poor outcomes is quite complex and is undoubtedly the result of the interaction of many factors for which we do not have a comprehensive empirical lens. Thus, their high levels of segregation may simply be a symptom of much larger systems failures. However, researchers have developed some important insights and interventions that can increase the likelihood that these children will be successful in school.

A major problem these students face in school is behaving within acceptable norms. A major aspect of their disability is often significant difficulty controlling behavior. Thus a major manifestation of their disability is likely to conflict with school discipline policies and practices.

Two leading researchers in this area, George Sugai and Rob Horner (2002), summarize the major principles upon which most school discipline codes are based:

> Most school conduct codes and discipline handbooks detail consequence sequences designed to "teach" these students that they have violated a school rule, and their "choice" of behavior will not be tolerated. When occurrences of rule-breaking behavior increase in frequency and intensity,
>
> a. monitoring and surveillance are increased to "catch" future occurrences of problem behavior,
> b. rules and sanctions for problem behavior are restated and reemphasized,

c. the continuum of punishment consequences for repeated rule violations is extended,

d. efforts are directed toward increasing the consistency with which school staff react to antisocial behavior,

e. "bottom line" consequences are accentuated to inhibit future displays of problem behavior. (p. 25)

Citing the work of a number of researchers, Sugai and Horner continue: "Ironically, when these types of solutions are used with the students with established histories of severe antisocial behavior, increases in intensity and frequency of antisocial behavior are likely" (2002, p. 25). As these antisocial activities increase, schools and districts frequently employ suspensions, expulsions, and movement to alternative programs, among other strategies. Though these responses are common, Sugai and Horner point out that they have not been adequately studied or validated.

Sugai and Horner go on to assert that these measures may create a false sense of security: "Environments of authoritarian control are established. Anti-social behavior events are inadvertently reinforced. Most importantly, the schools' primary function to provide opportunities for teaching and academic engagement is decreased" (p. 26).

The picture that emerges for many of these children under traditional discipline codes is one of frequent suspension and expulsion from school with the high risk of placement in an alternative program that may or may not have a more effective approach to their presenting behaviors. In a very real sense, these children are being required to be nondisabled in order to receive an effective education. Even students who may have the most intrinsically associated negative behaviors, such as those experienced by some students with autism, need concerted approaches designed to develop more socially appropriate behaviors if our goal is family and community participation.

The failure to respond to the needs of students with behavioral disabilities with interventions and supports that have been proven successful is another example of ableism. Students are often "punished" for behavior that arises out of their disability rather than being supported in changing their behavior. Traditional authoritarian approaches thus maximize the impact of these children while limiting their opportunities to participate. Over the years, the failure to provide for these children's needs may help explain the very poor outcomes these children often experience.

Some might interpret the failure of traditional discipline approaches as an argument for a more permissive approach to discipline for these students. However, it is important to note that these students are likely to experience bad life outcomes if their behavior does not change. Fortunately, a significant body of research has developed over the past two decades that has demonstrated that schools can deal more effectively with the behavior of these students while improving the overall learning climate. This research has involved a number of researchers who have worked collaboratively on federally funded research projects and have developed effective research-validated and universally designed school discipline and behavioral support systems. Prominent among these researchers are Hill Walker, George Sugai, and Rob Horner, all of the University of Oregon. Together, they and their colleagues have developed a schoolwide student discipline program referred to as Positive Behavior Intervention Support (PBIS).

PBIS is based on an extensive body of research that has demonstrated that effective behavioral systems developed for individual students can be taken beyond the individual student and be implemented within a whole-school approach, emphasizing collective behaviors, working structures, and standard routine approaches (Sugai & Horner, 2002). The key features of PBIS include

a. outcomes (e.g. academic achievement, social competence, employment options) that are uniquely defined and valued by stakeholders (e.g. students, families, teachers, employers),

b. a behavioral biomedical science of human behavior that provides fundamental principles for the design of support,

c. empirically validated practices for achieving identified outcomes in applied contexts,
d. the implementation of validated practices in the context of
   the systems change needed for durable effects. (p. 29)

Within this framework PBIS calls for school-tailored efforts supported by a strong leadership team guided by school-based data
and informed by research. It is important to reemphasize at this
point that students with the most significant behavioral issues will
need more than just schoolwide interventions. They will need
more individualized and specialized supports. However, efficient
schoolwide systems are essential for those who need the greatest
support. "A school's ability to implement an effective program for
the 3 percent to 7 percent of students with high risk behaviors,
those students likely to be labeled emotionally disturbed, is directly related to its capacity to provide a proactive schoolwide discipline program for the remaining student body" (Lewis & Sugai,
1999). Students with the greatest behavioral needs are thus not
well served in chaotic and poorly disciplined schools.

Sugai and Horner created a graphic representation of this principle (see Figure 1). According to Sugai, the PBIS approach is
being implemented in over 500 schools nationwide, and these
schools are systematically recording data (G. Sugai, personal
communication, August 2003). Some of these schools have experienced marked reductions in office discipline referrals of 50–
60 percent; at the same time, they have been able to focus in on
the most needy students. The following example illustrates this
point:

> However, one fourth-grade boy remained highly disruptive. His lewd
> comments and overactive behavior led to a recommendation for an
> alternative placement. Yet when the teacher assistance team con-
> ducted a functional behavioral assessment and started a self-man-
> agement program for the child, they noted a dramatic turnaround.
> The youngster's problem behaviors dropped by more than 80 per-
> cent, and he began completing academic assignments. The combi-

nation of the schoolwide system with targeted intervention for the individual child proved effective. (Horner et al., 2000, p. 21)

This research, coupled with the data showing widespread poor results for this population, prompted the inclusion in the IDEA of new significant requirements to proactively address the needs of these students (IDEA 1997, 300.346). It is not my intent here to discuss the PBIS program in great detail. This approach is relatively complex, and school personnel seeking to implement it should seek more informed guidance by going to the website for the OSEP-funded Center for Positive Behavioral Interventions and Supports (http://www.pbis.org). My goal here is to present this approach as a great example of how principles of universal design hold enormous promise for improving the education of students with behavioral disabilities. PBIS is clearly a program that recognizes both the specific needs of students with disabilities while promoting a more supportive overall learning environment in which their chances for success are improved. As such, it serves the goal that should underlie all education for students with disabilities by minimizing the impact of disability while maximizing students' opportunities to participate.

An innovative complement to the PBIS program for students with more significant behavioral problems is a system of "wraparound" services known as "systems of care" (Eber & Keenan, 2004). These programs are based on the need for children and families to be supported both in and out of schools in a comprehensive fashion. These programs seek "seamless" coordination between the school and outside agencies to meet the educational, mental health, and social services needs of children and families in a comprehensive and flexible manner. In one Illinois school district, these programs have been shown to be effective in reducing out-of-home settings and self-contained classrooms. A Rhode Island school district experienced decreases in truancies, suspensions, failing grades, and major aggressive episodes. Passing grades and school attendance increased (Eber & Keenan, 2004).

**FIGURE 1**
**Continuum of Schoolwide Instructional and Positive Behavioral Supports**

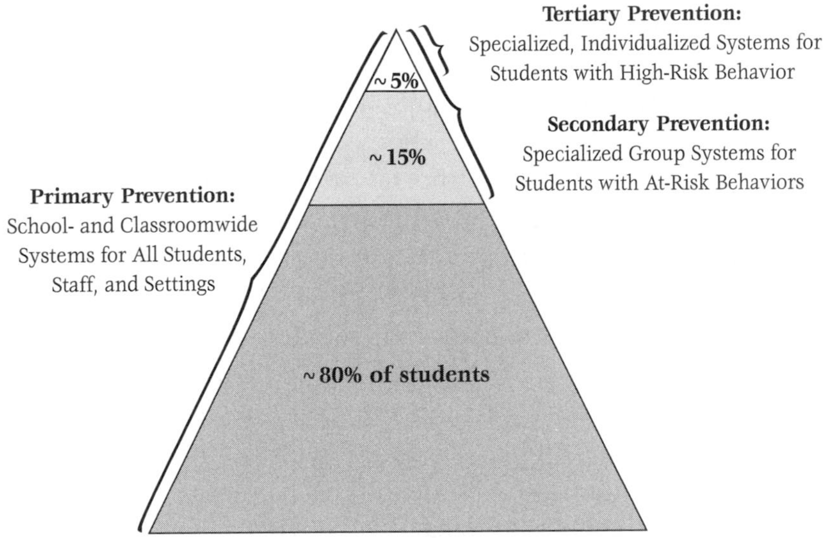

**Tertiary Prevention:**
Specialized, Individualized Systems for
Students with High-Risk Behavior

~5%

**Secondary Prevention:**
Specialized Group Systems for
Students with At-Risk Behaviors

~15%

**Primary Prevention:**
School- and Classroomwide
Systems for All Students,
Staff, and Settings

~80% of students

*Source:* Center on Positive Behavioral Interventions and Supports, Office of Special Education Programs, U.S. Department of Education, Washington, DC. Reprinted with permission.

The combination of PBIS with systems of care programs holds great promise for eliminating the ableist practices, discussed in chapter 1, that students with emotional disturbance experience. These programs recognize the needs that arise out of this disability and respond to them in a way that seeks to minimize the impact of disability while maximizing the opportunities for these children to be successful within their homes and communities. Further, these universally designed systems have potential benefit for other children as well.

## UNIVERSAL DESIGN AND SCHOOL ORGANIZATION

As the discussions of PBIS and reading instruction indicate, universal design may require significant organizational changes in schools. Some might argue that this is the classic case of the tail wagging the dog, even if there is clear benefit for all. Another line of scholarship—the work of school organization change scholars typified by Skrtic and Elmore—reinforces the force of the argument for universal design even further.

In his brilliant 1991 essay "The Special Education Paradox: Equity as the Way to Excellence," Thomas Skrtic deconstructed the practice of special education and its effort to integrate disabled children through PL 94-142 by applying organizational and critical theory. He concluded that, "from an organizational perspective, the basic problem with the EHA (PL 94-142) is that it attempts to force an adhocratic [collaborative problem-solving] value orientation on a professional bureaucracy by treating it as if it were a machine bureaucracy" (Skrtic, 1991, p. 172). In Skrtic's analysis the effective education of students with disabilities is uncertain work that requires a problem-solving type of organization in order to be effective, not a typical school where teachers, whether general or special, implement standard programs (a professional bureaucracy). Further, relying solely on a legalized structure (a machine bureaucracy) is insufficient to create the change needed at the student level for effective integrated education. Skrtic goes on to posit that student diversity is not a liability but rather a potential asset to schools that adopt problem-solving structures. "Regardless of its causes and its extent student diversity is not a liability in a problem solving organization; it is an asset, an enduring uncertainty, and thus the driving force behind innovation, growth of knowledge, and progress" (Skrtic, 1991, p. 177). He concludes, "In structural and cultural terms, school organizations cannot be adhocratic—and thus cannot be excellent, equitable, or democratic—without student diversity. In adhocratic school organization, educational equity is a precondition for educational excellence" (Skrtic, 1991, p. 179).

Skrtic's piece predated the application of the term "universal design" to schooling. Yet his writing clearly advocates the principles that would create the conditions under which children with disabilities and other diverse learners would be able to access schooling in a natural and effective manner. Further, his writing predates the more widespread inclusion of more significantly disabled students into general education classes. The successful integration of more significantly disabled students into general education classes has reinforced the central thesis of Skrtic's work.

Effective inclusive schools almost always implement nonstandard approaches that require problem solving from a variety of people with different perspectives and backgrounds, including parents. Further, we know the work is often uncertain. The successful inclusion of the autistic child discussed above in the section dealing with PBIS demonstrates that staff and students must constantly problem solve to successfully include a child with this disability. There is no standard program or "bureaucratic cookbook" that will produce an effective program for these children.

Good inclusive schools such as the O'Hearn School in Boston (Hehir & Gamm, 1999) have moved away from traditional structures and provide many opportunities for professionals to work together in classrooms to improve curriculum and instruction. Many of these schools have extended this approach to all students. There is emerging evidence that good, inclusive urban schools are among the best-performing schools in urban districts. Three inclusive schools in Boston, the O'Hearn, the Mason, and the Mary Lyons, all of which integrate students with significant disabilities into general education classrooms, have consistently scored well on academic measures (see http://BPS.k12.ma.us.gov, March 17, 2005). All of these schools employ collaborative organizational models. It seems increasingly evident that "command and control" centralized bureaucracies in special education may have been effective in putting processes and programs in place but are proving inadequate to the task of fundamental instructional improvement.

The literature in general education is also recognizing the inadequacy of traditional structures for improving educational performance within the era of standards-based reform. Richard Elmore's (2004) work is very insightful and fits nicely into the concept of universal design. His work has been heavily influenced by the successful school reform efforts he researched in the former District 2 in New York City. His principle of distributive leadership begins with defining "improvement" as the ability of an organization to demonstrate that it can make progress toward a goal by, among other things, "engaging people in analysis and understanding of why some actions seem to work and others don't" (p. 57). Elmore moves away from the traditional notions of heroic charismatic leaders and defines school leadership as the ability to guide instructional improvement. Teachers, those who deliver instruction, have the best grasp of how to improve instruction by guiding and providing direction. Though collaboration and collegiality are central to Elmore's theory of distributive leadership, they are insufficient in and of themselves. Leadership must seek to parcel out responsibility and authority for guiding instruction. Doing so increases the likelihood that the decisions of teachers and administrators will result in collective benefits in student learning. Elmore further asserts that standards-based reform creates the enabling context for all this.

Elmore's (2004) model of distributive leadership consists of two tasks: one involves describing the ground rules that leaders would have to follow to carry out large-scale improvement, the other describes how they will share responsibility. He goes on to generate principles for effective distributive leadership:

1. The purpose of leadership is to improve practice and performance.
2. Improvement requires continuous learning both by individuals and groups.
3. Leaders lead by exemplifying the values and behaviors they want others to adopt, meaning that leaders should expect to have their own practice subject to scrutiny.
4. People cooperate with one another in achieving their goals when they recognize other people's expertise.
5. Leaders are responsible for helping to make possible what they are requiring others to do.

Elmore emphasizes that the demands of standards-based reform require fundamental changes in the institutional practice and structure of public schools. In this context those in leadership roles have to be change agents who engage people in learning a new form of practice. Central to Elmore's work is the need for vastly improved professional development embedded in the work of teaching and learning. It is impossible to do justice here to Elmore's work other than to say that it adds additional support to the fundamental principles of universal design and the need for fundamental change in how we structure schools and in the work of improving teaching and learning for all students. Therefore, I highly recommend his most recent book, *School Reform from the Inside Out* (Elmore, 2004).

Looking at Elmore's and Skrtic's work together in the context of standards-based reform makes it clear that in order to provide more equitable and effective education for all students we will need to make fundamental changes in how we structure the work of schools. Though the challenge is significant, universally designed schools hold hope not only for students but also for teachers. The inclusive schools I cited in Boston all have no difficulty attracting and retaining teachers.

## CONCLUSION

Universal design is a promising concept that will flourish and evolve. Early applications of this concept to schooling are supportive of the overall goal of minimizing the impact of disability and maximizing the opportunities to participate. Universally designed schools allow disabled students to access education naturally. The needs that arise out of their disability become situated more within the environment in which they are functioning than within themselves. As such, they reinforce the fundamental message of this book that disability is a natural form of human diversity that is neither pitiable nor heroic, that disability is only tragic when the needs of disabled people are not met. The challenge, therefore, is to eliminate ableism by affirming the fundamental rights of disabled children to equitable quality education so that they may take their rightful place in the world. The next chapter addresses what may be the most significant major policy issue in the education of students with disabilities: the inclusion of students with disabilities in standards-based reform. The explicit goal of these policies reflected in IDEA 1997 and No Child Left Behind is to improve educational results for all students, including those with disabilities. As such, it holds much hope for eliminating the pervasive ableist attitude that children with disabilities are incapable.

# 5

# Students with Disabilities and Standards-Based Reform

A disability advocate recently sought my advice on the placement of an eight-year-old student with disabilities. The boy has various communication and motor disabilities due to brain damage at birth. He has received excellent early intervention and preschool services. His speech, though labored, is easily understood, and his vocabulary approximates that of peers his age. He has some difficulties in coordination, fine motor skills, and behavior but is not significantly cognitively impaired. Unfortunately, his current school placement is woefully inadequate. At his individualized education program (IEP) meeting, his mother asked what he was learning in science. She wanted to make sure he was being prepared to take the statewide assessment in grade four. The special education teacher responded, "We're not doing science. We're concentrating on fine motor development." Again, like that of too many children with disabilities, this boy's educational program concentrates inordinately on the characteristics of his disability at the expense of access to the curriculum.

This example illustrates why many disability advocates view standards-based educational reforms as holding great promise to help eradicate the most insidious ableist assumption: that people with disabilities are not intellectually capable. The education of students with disabilities has been plagued by low expectations, which is why many in the disability community have sought to have students included in state and national accountability systems (Thurlow, 2000). The hope is that by including students in statewide assessments, more attention will be paid to assuring that these students receive quality programs (McDonnell et al., 1997). In 1997, advocates were successful in getting the Individuals with Disabilities Education Act (IDEA) amended to require students with disabilities to be included in statewide assessments. The No Child Left Behind Act (NCLB), as well as the 2004 reauthorization of the IDEA, expanded these provisions by requiring significantly greater accountability.

It is noteworthy that, before this federal requirement, most states excluded most students with disabilities from these important accountability systems at a time when most states were implementing various forms of standards-based reform (Thurlow, 2000). I recall a meeting I had with the former secretary of education, Richard Riley, in 1994. The secretary asked me how the students with disabilities had performed on the National Assessment of Educational Progress (NAEP). I told him I could not answer his inquiry because, by and large, the disabled students had been excluded. He was a bit incredulous and then responded, "We'll have to change that."

A number of explanations may address this exclusion. It is possible that disabled students were viewed as not capable of achieving standards. Another explanation might be that the performance of disabled students was not considered important enough to track. Both of these explanations clearly reflect ableist attitudes, that disabled students are either incapable or unimportant.

Another explanation is that in high-stakes environments school districts may actually be placing more students in special education to avoid accountability (Allington & McGill-Franzen, 1989) or, as I experienced as associate superintendent of schools in Chicago in the early nineties, because of their fear of the assumed negative impact on aggregate scores that would result from inclusion. When I was in Chicago I tried, unsuccessfully, to get students with disabilities into the local assessment. The district would not risk the public relations fallout that would have ensued if test scores went down.

A more positive reason for this exclusion might be that states simply have not known how to accommodate students with disabilities in assessments. There are many technical issues involved in the inclusion of students with disabilities, especially those who receive accommodations (Koretz & Hamilton, 2000). Though the truth probably lies somewhere among these views, the exclusion of students with disabilities from state and local assessment systems may result in their exclusion from the curriculum and thus reinforce the status quo of low expectations, leaving students with disabilities seriously undereducated. Fortunately, this exclusion is now illegal.

Though there was widespread exclusion of students with disabilities from statewide accountability systems before the passage of the 1997 amendments to the IDEA, some states had begun to implement inclusive policies prior to the federal requirement. These states provide an interesting window on the impact of these policies. Increasing evidence indicates that inclusion in statewide assessment may be improving the educational opportunities of students with disabilities.

In New York State, where an emphasis on including students with disabilities in the Regents Exam began in 1998, the number of students passing this high-level test has greatly increased. A comparison of the data from 1997 and 2000 shows dramatic change. In 1997, only 4,419 students with disabilities took the Regents English Exam, with 3,414 passing. Three years later, over twice as many disabled students *passed* the test as had taken it in 1997. In 2000, 13,528 took the test, and 9,514 passed (New York State Department of Education, 2001). Prior to this inclusionary push, some school districts in the state did not have *one* student with disabilities taking the test. It appears that in these school districts, the view was indeed ableist; no child with disabilities was viewed as capable of passing this test. The impact of the exclusion of students with disabilities from the Regents over the years was undoubtedly significant. Important benefits can result from passing the Regents, from scholarships to college admissions. Further, the widespread exclusion from the Regents prior to 1997 probably meant that thousands of students with disabilities did not take higher-level high school courses.

In Maryland, where students with disabilities have been included in the state's basic skills test, many districts have shown steady progress to the point where the vast majority of students with disabilities are passing the test. Maryland has years of disaggregated performance data. These data were used to help negotiate an agreement to end a long-standing class-action suit concerning students with disabilities in Baltimore City. This agreement broke new ground in that it focused on educational outcomes (*Vaughn, G., et al. v. Mayor and City Council of Baltimore, et al.*, 2000). The previous agreement, like many special education class-action suits, had focused largely on processes (Hehir & Gamm, 1999) and made no mention of academic performance in any area. Though the agreement went into effect in the 2000–01 school year, and thus it is too soon to evaluate its impact, the city's special education director speaks positively of how the agreement is focusing staff on teaching and learning (G. Amos, personal communication, 2001; see also Sabel & Simon, 2004).[1]

A more recent report in May 2004 compiled by the National Center on Educational Outcomes, which is funded by the Office of Special Education Programs of the U.S. Department of Education

---

1. Sabel and Simon (2004) assert that the agreement in *Vaughn G.* represents a larger trend in public litigation from a model of top-down, command-and-control bureaucracy toward one involving "stakeholder negotiation, continuously revised performance measures, and transparency" (p. 1016).

(DOE), documented positive consequences for students with disabilities resulting from their inclusion in large-scale assessment and accountability systems (Ysseldyke et al., 2004). This study utilized primarily qualitative methodologies, including analysis of focus group data, reports in the media, and reports from state officials, coupled with some quantitative data. The report gives a very positive impression of the results stemming from the inclusion of students with disabilities in these state systems. The positive results reported include markedly increased participation rates of students with disabilities in assessments, higher expectations for students, improved instruction, improved performance, increased collaboration between special education and general education, and positive portrayals of students with disabilities within the media.

Examples of improvements cited in this report include an increase in test scores in several states. Louisiana reported increased pass rates on its high-stakes exam in 2000–01 with fourth-grade students with disabilities increasing by 9 percent in math and 5 percent in English. Virginia reported average gains from 3 to 5 percent in the same year. Colorado reported significant improvement over time from 1997 to 2001, with fourth-grade performance improving 107 percent; one third of students with disabilities were meeting state standards in reading. California reading scores for students with disabilities have increased steadily since 1998 despite the relatively stagnant performance of the general education population (Ysseldyke et al., 2004).

It is important to view these initial findings with a bit of caution. First, state standards vary widely from state to state. Therefore, these data do not constitute solid evidence of national improvement in student outcomes. Further, states may change their proficiency standards over time, making longitudinal comparisons invalid. Finally, improved pass rates may represent relatively small increments in actual student learning if large numbers of students have moved from just below the passing level to just above. This being said, the preponderance of the evidence reported by Ysseldyke and colleagues is indeed positive, and other evidence confirms this assertion.

## THE CASE OF MASSACHUSETTS

Massachusetts provides an interesting case for examining the inclusion of students with disabilities for a number of reasons. First, for more than ten years the state has engaged in a school improvement process that has sought to unite curriculum frameworks that represent high standards with capacity building and opportunities to learn (Reville, 2004). Second, the state performs at or close to the top on the NAEP and above average on the SAT, with many above average participation rates. Thus, the state can claim success using relatively objective external benchmarks. Third, the state adopted inclusive policies in 1993, four years before the federal requirement. Fourth, Massachusetts is relatively diverse, with significant populations of racial, linguistic minorities and low-income students. Finally, some interesting research is available concerning the participation of students with disabilities that provides a potentially useful lens with which to assess this policy.

Students in Massachusetts must pass exams in order to graduate with a diploma. This high-stakes exam is first administered in tenth grade, and students can take the test repeatedly during high school until they pass it. The test is also administered in both fourth and eighth grades. Though no stakes are attached to the child as a result of the test at these levels, the tests are used to determine school-level accountability under No Child Left Behind. The state allows a rather robust set of accommodations for students with disabilities.

It would be hard not to be impressed with Massachusetts's results. In the graduating class of 2003, 90 percent of disabled students passed English, 83 percent passed mathematics, and 85 percent passed both (Reville, 2004). This is a marked improvement over the performance of students with disabilities in 1999, when

75 percent failed the English test and 87 percent failed the math (Massachusetts Department of Education, 2005).

It should be emphasized that these exams are quite difficult, and passing them represents a significant level of proficiency. (Readers can judge for themselves by visiting the Massachusetts Department of Education website, where sample items are provided.) The fact that so many students with disabilities are meeting these standards contradicts the ableist assumption of inferiority. Further, achieving this level of competency will undoubtedly increase options for these students in higher education and employment.

Though this performance is impressive, a look behind the data may lead to some caution. I conducted a study with three of my colleagues in the context of a class-action suit regarding state funding of low-income districts that I believe provides important findings relevant to the participation of students with disabilities in high-stakes testing. The study raises serious questions about whether students attending low-income districts in Massachusetts are being given the opportunities to learn that increase the likelihood that they will be able to pass the exam (Hehir et al., 2003). I discuss this research in detail not just because of its relevance to the discussion of standards-based reform but also because the methodology we used may be useful to assess whether school districts are implementing practices associated with enabling disabled students to achieve better outcomes.

This case grew out of a request for me to serve as an expert witness in a school finance case in Massachusetts, *Hancock v. Driscoll.* The case involves student plaintiffs from 19 low-resource school districts who claim that they were not receiving the standard of education required by the state constitution. This case builds on an earlier case, *McDuffy v. Secretary of Executive Office of Education*, in which the Massachusetts Supreme Judicial Court found the state in violation of its constitution. The court concluded that the state had an obligation to educate all its children and held that children in less affluent communities "are not receiving their constitutional entitlement of education as intended by the framers of the Constitution." The court further required the state to define the standard of education that the commonwealth must provide.

In response to the *McDuffy* decision, the state legislature passed and the governor signed the Education Reform Act of 1993, which, among other important provisions, established a "foundation budget" for each school district to be phased in over seven years (Massachusetts General Laws, 1993, chap. 69). This act also included extra resources for students deemed "at risk." *Hancock v. Driscoll,* a new case, is rooted in the McDuffy decision as a result of a motion for relief filed in 1999. This led to a determination that a trial court will rely on the state's curriculum standards to judge the constitutionality of the education provided to the students in the plaintiff districts. The plaintiffs asserted that, despite the provisions of the Education Reform Act of 1993, students continue to be denied their state constitutional rights due to, among other things, lack of appropriate facilities, unqualified teaching staffs, inordinately large class sizes, and lack of access to technology. According to the plaintiffs, these problems are due to a lack of adequate resources within these districts.

I was asked to determine if students with disabilities were being given access to appropriate educational options, and, if they were not, were financial resources partly responsible for the breakdown. This question gave rise to an evaluation design that provided interesting findings concerning the disparities in educational opportunities available to students in poorer districts during the era of standards-based education.

We (Hehir et al., 2003) approached the task of determining whether students were receiving access to the curriculum standards and making sufficient progress toward the attainment of such standards by asking the following question: What would we expect to see happening within these schools if children with disabilities were receiving effective education based on the best available research? We developed a framework that includes four standards of practice upon which we could evaluate the implementation of special education. This framework is very consistent with the ideas put forth in this book. They are:

1. Children who demonstrate potential problems with reading and/or behavior should be identified and supported at an early age, prior to referral for special education services.
2. The process for special education referral should be appropriate, culturally sensitive, timely, and efficient.
3. Students with disabilities should be educated in the least restrictive environment and have access to the general curriculum.
4. The educational outcomes of students with disabilities, defined here as passing the Massachusetts Comprehensive Assessment System (MCAS), with the exception of those with cognitive disabilities, should be comparable to those of their nondisabled peers.

These four standards parallel the three stages of the special education process—*prereferral*, *referral*, and the *provision of services*—and a fourth stage or, rather, consequence of the first three stages—*student outcomes*. These four standards are intimately linked, and we argue that an effective framework for evaluation should not only look at evidence of effectiveness within each standard but should also look for how each standard connects with and builds upon the others. The first three standards implemented properly also serve to minimize disability while maximizing opportunities to participate. The first standard is an example of the importance of universal design discussed in chapter 4.

### Findings

In our evaluation for *Hancock v. Driscoll*, we found in general that, in the four low-income districts, practices were not consistent with the standards upon which this evaluation was based and that there was a connection between lack of available resources and implementation of the standards. In contrast, we further found rather high implementation of these standards in the high-income districts. This study thus painted a "tale of two cities" picture of special education implementation. In high-income communities students largely benefit from research-based, state-of-the-art practices, with the vast majority passing a rather difficult state exit exam. On the other hand, students with disabilities in low-income districts receive late interventions, poor access to the general curriculum, and significantly higher levels of segregation, with the great majority failing to pass exit exams and thus risking a life without the benefits of a high school diploma.

We found that by engaging in a rigorous and in-depth examination of how and why these standards were not being met we were able to reveal complexities that were quite informative not only for the purposes of the lawsuit but for the districts themselves. In fact, one of the districts decided to use our findings as part of a larger self-improvement effort within the district. What follows are two examples of findings from our study that demonstrate how students with disabilities are not being given access to appropriate opportunities to learn, are not receiving appropriate preferral interventions, and are not being educated in the least restrictive environment (LRE).

In general, we found that the low-income districts were not providing adequate support for children who demonstrated problems with reading or behavior in the early grades. Moreover, our qualitative data helped us to understand *why* these practices were not occurring. Specifically, our interviews revealed that although leadership personnel knew they should be intervening with children who demonstrated problems with reading or behavior, they reported that they did not have sufficient resources to do so. For example, the special education director in one district explained that the district did not provide robust literacy instruction in general education; rather, special education provided most of the literacy remediation. She hypothesized that more students were referred for special education services than would have been if the district provided these services. The one low-income district that did provide rather systematic early intervention for students expe-

**FIGURE 1**

**Percentage of Special Education Students Classified as "Failing" on the ELA and Mathematics Components of the MCAS in Grades 4 and 10, by District: 2002**

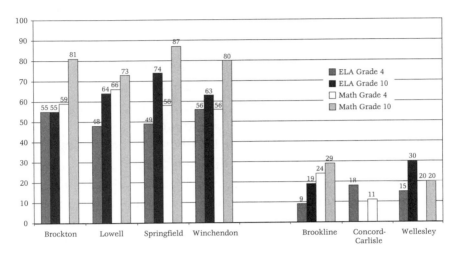

*Note:* Low-income communities are Brockton, Lowell, Springfield, and Winchendon.

riencing reading difficulties did so primarily through various grant resources. The "entrepreneurial" leaders of this district expressed concern that these efforts could not continue if they were not able to bring in these funds.

There were other examples of variability in prereferral practices among the low-income districts, indicating that resources alone were not the only factor involved. One of the low-income districts we evaluated had fewer students classified as seriously emotionally disturbed (SED) (7%) than the national average (8.2%). We found that the district had a solid program of behavioral interventions in general education used prior to a special education referral. Through interviews with district administration, we learned that before a student is referred for special education services for behavior, the district employs what it terms a "three-level triage," which helps school personnel identify those students with a "conduct disorder" and those with an emotional disability. These interventions may help explain why the district had fewer students classified as SED than the national average.

Concerning the issue of LRE and access, we found that, though there was a good deal of variability, the students in the low-income districts were far more likely to be placed in more restrictive educational settings than their counterparts in more affluent districts. For instance, one district educated only 24 percent of its students with disabilities in regular classes, 54 percent of its students with disabilities in resource rooms, and 11 percent of its students with disabilities in separate classrooms.

Our methodology allowed us to look beyond these numbers to understand why the district had difficulty educating its students with disabilities in regular classrooms. We found that leaders and staff in the district wanted very much to practice inclusion to the greatest degree possible but just did not have the resources to do so in a way that would be effective. For example, inclusion requires a collaborative relationship between special education and general education teachers that allows students with disabilities to receive both access to the general education curriculum and individualized support. In this district, schools were greatly understaffed. As a result, the most efficient way to serve students with disabilities was to educate them for most of the day in a resource room. When they went into the regular classroom, they rarely had support from a special education teacher. In addition, there was no money to provide professional training for regular education teachers on how to provide appropriate accommodations or modifications and access to the general education curriculum.

Those schools that were able to educate students with disabilities for most of the day in a regular classroom were forced to "cluster" all the students with disabilities in one class because of their limited staff. One principal told us: "Ideally, . . . you want to divide them evenly in classes, but we have to cluster them together in order to use our limited special education staff efficiently. But then, is that really [inclusion]? It's not really following the letter of their IEP. But we do the best we can. We compromise."

**TABLE 1**
**Percentage of Time Students with Disabilities**
**Spend in Different Educational Environments**

| | Educational Environment | | | | |
|---|---|---|---|---|---|
| | Regular Class (%) | Resource Room (%) | Separate Class (%) | Separate Building (%) | Private Day (%) |
| Hancock Districts | | | | | |
| Brockton | 58 | 14 | 16 | 2 | 3 |
| Lowell | 24 | 54 | 11 | 0.5 | 3 |
| Springfield | 44 | 19 | 24 | 1 | 6 |
| Winchendon | 53 | 16 | 11 | 4 | 2 |
| Comparison Districts | | | | | |
| Brookline | 73 | 10 | 7 | 2 | 1 |
| Concord-Carlisle | 37 | 44 | 1 | 7 | 8 |
| Wellesley | 75 | 6 | 5 | 0 | 4 |
| Massachusetts State Average | 65 | 14 | 14 | 2 | 3 |

Note: The categories of "regular class" and "resource room" are defined differently for federal versus Massachusetts state standards. The Massachusetts state averages were taken from federally collected data and therefore follow those standards. The data for Brockton, Lowell, Springfield, and Winchendon, on the other hand, were collected using the Massachusetts state standards. Federal standards define "regular class" as less than 21 percent of the school day outside of the regular classroom and "resource room" as between 21 and 60 percent of the school day outside of the regular classroom. Massachusetts state standards define "regular class" as less than 25 percent of the school day outside of the regular classroom and "resource room" as between 25 and 60 percent of the school day outside of the regular classroom.

For most of the schools in this district clustering was not even an option. Without adequate support from special education teachers, students with disabilities could not effectively access the general education curriculum in a regular education class.

Furthermore, nearly all of the students with emotional disabilities in this district were placed in self-contained classrooms. These students require staff with a specialized expertise, of which there was an extreme shortage. We found an average of 1 psychologist to 230 students with disabilities in the four low-income districts we looked at, compared to 1 to 95 in the high-income districts. The ability to provide high-quality services to this population was therefore heavily compromised in the low-income districts, in turn leading to even greater difficulty in providing services in the least restrictive environment.

The picture that emerges from this study is that the education of children with disabilities in these low-income districts departs significantly from practices that would increase the likelihood that they will pass the MCAS and thus minimize the impact of disability. And, in Massachusetts, this means that large numbers of these students will be denied diplomas. The good news is that in the high-income communities, where fidelity to best practices was rather high, virtually all noncognitively disabled students with disabilities appear to pass these tests. Thus, this research corresponds with the study done by Ysseldyke and colleagues (2004) that highlighted one suburban Minnesota community where only 3 of the 182 seniors did not pass the exit exam (p. 16). It is important to add here that school achievement is highly correlated with socioeconomic status, and thus the achievement of high-income students is likely influenced by their family income. However, that makes it even more important that schools that enroll large numbers of low-income students implement practices that can overcome these differences. As Reville (2004) states,

> Poverty is a powerful and persistent obstacle to learning. Standards-based reformers acknowledge the injury of poverty, but they reject the temptation to give up on children by declaring "poverty as destiny." Instead, we embrace the strategies needed to make education truly matter in improving the prospects of those born into economic disadvantage. As a nation, we make a gigantic investment in schooling. We have an obligation to expect and deliver results. We know that education has been a ladder out of poverty for many. Our challenge is to make that ladder work for everyone. Our goal must be to get the conditions of teaching and learning right for each and every student. (p. 596)

Unfortunately, though the judge in the *Hancock* case, Margot Bosford, found in favor of the plaintiffs, the Supreme Judicial Court of Massachusetts reversed her decision. The court found that Massachusetts had made sufficient progress in addressing funding inequities. Though this was unfortunate, the study documents serious implementation issues related to high-stakes testing and low-income disabled students that require significant attention if the districts involved in this study can be expected to meet the requirements of NCLB. Undoubtedly, other low-income districts face similar challenges. More important, these students risk not graduating with a diploma but going through life without an adequate education.

## STUDENT PERCEPTIONS OF HIGH-STAKES TESTING

Another research study that provides additional important information about standards-based reform in Massachusetts was a dissertation conducted by Lauren Katzman (2004). Katzman conducted a qualitative study involving a sample of 24 students with disabilities and 12 students without disabilities in two urban high schools in Massachusetts. She conducted extensive interviews and developed in-depth cases for each student concerning how he or she experienced the tenth-grade MCAS exam. The vast majority of Katzman's subjects were minority and poor. Specifically, she collected data on how students felt about the exam, how they reacted to either passing or failing it, how test performance affected their motivation and whether it influenced the likelihood of their dropping out of school, whether students felt academically prepared, their understanding of their disabilities and the accommodations they may have been given. Her research provides interesting insights into how students with disabilities, who are most likely to suffer negative consequences from high-stakes testing policy, will likely be affected by these policies. Her findings are relevant to educators and policy makers and provide another lens for examining the Massachusetts experience.

Katzman's research, like so much qualitative research, provides a complex picture. Though only two of the students with disabilities passed both the English and mathematics sections of the tenth-grade test (8%), with five (21%) passing only English and five (21%) passing only mathematics on their first attempt, the students in her study by and large persisted and participated in help sessions. (The nondisabled students passed both tests at a 67 percent rate, while 75 percent passed only English and 75 percent passed only mathematics.) Though five members of the disability sample eventually dropped out, the persistence of most of the students is noteworthy. MCAS seemed to increase their motivation to work hard in school. Further, the decision to drop out of school was not likely to be due to MCAS alone, as many of these students had experienced other events in their lives that also increased their risks, such as high levels of earlier retention and chronic absenteeism. Indeed, one of the students who passed the MCAS dropped out.

There are a number of findings in Katzman's study that illustrate how these students experience this policy as well as how practices that schools engage in may increase the chances that students either succeed or fail. An important finding in Katzman's study is that most of these students view the burden of passing the MCAS as falling solely on them. Though this may increase their motivation to work harder in school, some of Katzman's interviewees seethed with anger when they discussed how their schools have not prepared them for the test. The notion of shared responsibility between students and schools for achieving higher standards incorporated in legislation like No Child Left Behind, with its school-based adequate yearly progress standard, or the IDEA's state improvement requirements has not been communicated to the students.

A particularly important finding in this study is the fact that most students with disabilities felt unprepared to take the tenth-grade test because they had not been taught the curriculum, particularly in mathematics. The students' perception was supported by Katzman's transcript review, which revealed that only half the students with disabilities had taken any geometry prior to taking MCAS the first time. (This was true of 25 percent of the nondisabled sample.) Some of the students with disabilities attributed their lack of preparedness to being in special education classes.

> If you been in special ed since you was in ninth through twelfth grade and you took the test, I doubt you be having a clue what you had on there. . . . Because in special ed they teach you like more of a easier-level like stuff, like things, so you can get more, but like by the time you get up to pace with everybody you're still gonna be far back on the things that you missed. *So you're saying in special ed they do easier work?* Like, compared to MCAS, yeah. It's like we're catching up to what everybody's learning, and by the time we catch up we're still learning the things, and when you have to take the MCAS you're still learning and you don't know what—you gotta learn all of it, and there's like still stuff that is still need to be taught. (Katzman, 2004, p. 125)

It appears that for these students, the assignment to special education classes resulted in a lack of access to important curriculum. Though it is important to avoid conclusions from such small samples, these findings indicate that special class placements may be accentuating the impact of the students' disabilities.

Another important finding in Katzman's study is the perception students have toward the availability of help to pass the test at their schools. The two schools in Katzman's study varied significantly, with the students attending one school receiving significant help in passing the test, while those attending the other school expressed frustration over the lack of availability or quality of help. At the school with more support, students described a systematic program of supplemental support that was confirmed by Katzman's observations at the school and her analysis of school records. At this school, students who failed MCAS enrolled in at least one of a combination of four sections designed to help them pass the tests. One student described his experience: "They help us understand like all the big words. They help us understand a little better. . . . We had to read books about MCAS. . . . Another teacher I had was Mr. C. . . . He taught us like all the parts of math for the MCAS. So, now I can ace the math part on the MCAS" (Katzman, 2004, p. 137).

At this school all the students with disabilities who failed the MCAS took one of these courses. Though the number of students in this study is insufficient to allow us to draw conclusions about the impact of supplemental help, it should be noted that the students with disabilities passed at higher rates. The other school enrolled only 23 percent of the disabled students in supplemental programs. This contrasts with a participation rate of 100 percent for those students without disabilities in Katzman's study who attended the first school. A student at the less-supportive school expressed her view: "If you wanted to go you could go, but—you know what I'm saying? They—no, nobody forced you" (Katzman, 2004, p. 140).

Another interesting finding in Katzman's research had to do with test accommodations. Though a review of school records revealed that almost all the students with disabilities had some form of accommodation, they were for the most part unaware of their accommodations. This finding is disturbing from a "self-determination" perspective. The lack of understanding these students have of their accommodations means it is highly unlikely that these students have developed the understanding of their disability they will need in order to advocate for themselves in the future. Again, this is likely to result in their disabilities having a greater impact on their future prospects. For instance, if one of these students needs additional time on a civil service exam, he is unlikely to get it unless he can advocate for himself. It should be noted that in a recent program evaluation of a suburban high school's special education program I conducted with Katzman and two other colleagues, we found that the students with disabilities in this affluent school had a deep understanding of the nature of their disabilities and the accommodations they needed (Hehir et al., 2003). Again, this seems to reinforce the findings in our *Hancock* study that special education implementation is significantly more effective in more affluent districts than in poorer ones.

Finally, another interesting finding in Katzman's research may seem a bit paradoxical. That is, for two of her subjects, passing the MCAS may have served to keep them in school when otherwise they may have dropped out. Though her numbers are far too small to draw conclusions, this clearly is an area for future research. One student summed up these feelings well:

> I was scared to take it, cause I know if I wasn't gonna take it I was gonna go to Job Corps, and I was like, I'd rather go to get—I'd rather get my high-school diploma than go to Job Corps, know what I'm saying? And that's for me—that's what motivated me to do my work more, cause I had to pass the MCAS too, and I know if I was—if I didn't pass the MCAS and I just did my work, I wasn't gonna get my high-school diploma, I was just gonna get a certificate after all the work I done did. So what I did was I took the—I did the MCAS first, and passed the MCAS, then after that, know what I'm saying, I got my high-school diploma. I don't gotta go to Job Corps no more. I was gonna go. I was scared. I didn't think I could pass it, but I did. (Katzman, 2004, p. 170)

The other student for whom passing the MCAS seemed to have a similar effect expressed his new sense of improved self-perception: "It makes me feel smarter, that's, that's how I feel. Not saying that they're dumb or whatever, I'm just saying. I'm ain't trying to say I'm smarter than everybody, you know what I'm saying I'm just saying that makes me feel I'm smart" (Katzman, 2004, p. 170). It appears that these students had accepted a view of themselves that they were less than capable. Thus, they may have internalized ableist attitudes from their surroundings.

As should be clear from the discussion thus far, the inclusion of students with disabilities in statewide assessments and accountability systems shows much promise. Large numbers of students with disabilities appear to be experiencing improved educational outcomes that may not have happened without these policies. For these successful students, large-scale accountability may be helping to eliminate the ableist assumption of low expectations and will likely serve to open the doors of future opportunity. This is a significant policy victory. Further, it appears that future progress is likely to occur as NCLB is implemented. The *Boston Globe* reported that members of the school committee in one Massachusetts town were quite upset over the fact that their district was deemed as in need of improvement because of the performance of students with disabilities on the statewide assessment. "It's really frustrating to have that label because of one subgroup," one board member said (Schworm, 2004a). Also, the superintendent of the Boston Public Schools recently conducted a high-profile, districtwide study both to better understand the poor performance of students with disabilities on the MCAS and to identify effective practices within the system. This attention to the performance of students with disabilities is long overdue and has been hailed by advocates. "This isn't a new problem. In many schools this has been the reality for a long time. . . . We're just learning about it," said Richard Robison, executive director of the Federation for Children with Special Needs (Schworm, 2004a).

However, as the Massachusetts case demonstrates, a number of equity issues continue. Primary among these is the lack of access to opportunities to learn, particularly for students who come from low-income environments. The imposition of high-stakes policies on students who have not received appropriate opportunities to learn is, in my view, problematic. Further, it is likely that for some students the imposition of high-stakes testing without appropriate preparation will increase already high dropout rates.

Also, it should be noted that though Massachusetts has made significant progress in getting the great majority of students over the bar, many other states have yet to reach the point where a majority of their students with disabilities are passing the large-scale assessments. Therefore, though progress may be happening, many students are not experiencing it, and they will suffer the high-stakes consequences such as retention in grade or failure to qualify for a high school diploma. Though the strategy of applying high-stakes consequences to performance on these tests may be increasing performance averages among disabled students, the same policies may be having a very negative effect on individual students. That being said, the Massachusetts experience seems to demonstrate that significant progress can occur over time. Further, it is likely that much more progress could be made if all students with disabilities were given true opportunities to learn and if appropriate accommodations were made available to them. As Massachusetts has demonstrated, the vast majority of students with noncognitive disabilities can pass a high-content state exam.

## ADDITIONAL CONCERNS REGARDING STANDARDS-BASED REFORMS

In order to understand the potential impact of standards-based reforms at the local level or for an individual child, it is important to understand the local and state policy context. Each state has a good deal of latitude in crafting its statewide accountability systems. In some states local school districts have flexibility as well. Therefore, in order to assess the likely impact of state-level standards-based policy on children with disabilities, states implement one of four types of standards-based reform accountability measures (Katzman, 2001). One type is low content standard, low stakes. In these states the accountability system is based on a relatively low-content-level test with minimal stakes applied to students. This mode is rapidly disappearing. The second mode is low content, high stakes. That is, students may be denied promotion or a diploma if they fail to pass a relatively low-level test. The third type of implementation mode is high content, low stakes. This test assesses a rather high level of proficiency, yet the consequences do not result automatically in denial of grade promotion or graduation. Finally, the fourth type of policy is high content, high stakes, such as that of Massachusetts. This is rapidly becoming the dominant policy mode ("Count Me In," 2004). Under this type of policy students are denied either promotion or graduation due to their performance on a high-content-level statewide test.

Sometimes local school districts add requirements above and beyond state-level requirements. For instance, a local school district may have a high-stakes promotion policy, while the state has only a high-stakes graduation policy. Therefore, it is important to assess the policy environment in order to understand its potential impact on children and to plan for their success.

As previously emphasized, though the inclusion of students with disabilities in statewide assessments shows great promise, the imposition of high-stakes consequences for students who do not perform well on these tests gives rise to serious concerns. This is particularly the case when state policy requires the passage of high-level tests in order to receive a diploma or to move from grade to grade. One basic concern involves technical issues concerning construct validity; that is, do these tests measure accurately what students know and are able to do?

The inclusion of students with disabilities in accountability testing is complicated given the nature of disability and the type of assessments most states employ. Many disabled students require accommodations specific to their disability. For instance, blind children may require Braille administration of a test. Other children may require extra time due to very slow reading rates as a result of dyslexia. For students with disabilities these accommodations must be carefully chosen, and they should provide these students with equal access to the test. In principle, accommodations should provide students with a differential bounce; that is, the accommodation they receive should provide improved performance that would not have occurred without it and would not result in improved performance for a nondisabled student. There is evidence that accommodation decisions for students with disabilities are not done as thoughtfully as they could and that the concept of differential bounce is not widely employed. Further, the wrong accommodation may actually depress performance for some disabled students. For instance, extra time on a test may not be beneficial for a student with attentional difficulties. Large print may be detrimental for a student with tunnel vision. Therefore, it is important for educators and parents to make appropriate decisions around accommodations to assure that the test accurately measures student ability.

Another concern regarding the use of accommodations in the inclusion of students with disabilities in standards-based reforms has to do with construct validity. Does the accommodated administration of the test accurately measure what the test is designed to measure (Fuchs & Fuchs, 1999; Koretz & Hamilton, 2000)? For instance, a test that seeks to determine if a child can read print is invalidated if the test is read to the child. On the other hand, a math test may be invalid if it is not read to a child who is print-disabled because the child has no way to demonstrate the math she knows if she has to read print to do so. The issues of construct validity are complex, and, given the relative lack of experience in including disabled students in large-scale assessments, significant research will be required before we can be confident that these assessments accurately measure what students know and are able to do (Koretz & Hamilton, 2000).

Though there are numerous unresolved technical issues involved in including students with disabilities in assessments, high-stakes decisions are being made that have the potential to deny students important opportunities such as promotion or graduation. Further, beyond the technical issues is the nature of the constructs themselves. A major concern is whether the constructs are sufficiently broad to enable disabled students to demonstrate what they know and are able to do. A case that came to my attention when I was working at the DOE illustrates this point. The case involved a student who had become blind during high school. Although he was beginning to learn Braille, he was using taped books as his main means of learning from print. The state policies required all students to pass a test to graduate. The issue was whether he could participate in the language arts test through a taped administration. One of the constructs to be evaluated by this test was the ability to read print. He could not read print because he could not see print. Of course, he was not the only blind child in the state, and state policy allowed the state test to be administered in Braille. This boy, however, was not a proficient Braille reader because he was newly blind. The state decided to waive its policy that prohibited reading the language arts test aloud as an allowable accommodation for this student.

This example goes to the heart of the issues of construct validity, accommodations, and ableist assumptions regarding acceptable performance modes. The fundamental question here is, What is reading? The state had previously answered the question that reading was reading print or reading Braille. Extracting meaning from recorded text was not considered reading. Therefore, the statewide test was designed to measure these two modes of reading. Answering comprehension questions based on listening to recorded text would thus violate the construct validity of the test. However, significant numbers of disabled people use recorded text as their reading mode. These include people with a range of disabilities beyond blindness, including people who have dyslexia and people with certain types of cerebral palsy that make focusing on and reading print exhausting and inefficient. Joe Ford, for example, uses taped books for this reason. Even though the use of recorded text is widespread, some states refuse to allow taped administration of language arts tests, thereby refusing to recognize the mode that many disabled people use to read. Applying this narrow definition of reading to high-stakes decisions may mean that large numbers of disabled students will be denied diplomas and thus future educational opportunities. Further, such a decision is likely to discourage the use of taped texts in schools, even though they may represent the most efficient means by which some students with disabilities gain access to the curriculum. This decision runs the risk of increasing the impact of disability for the students involved.

Even if states broadly define modes of performance and successfully deal with measurement issues around construct validity, another issue is arising in states that have high-level-content, high-stakes assessment programs, that is, the problem of students who are incapable of passing the high-stakes tests due to the nature of their disability. This is particularly true of students with cognitive disabilities or mental retardation. Though it is important to have high expectations for all students, if states or local districts have diploma or promotion policies that assume the mastery of high levels of skill and knowledge, students with mental retardation, due to the pervasive nature of their significantly subaverage intellectual functioning, may be subject to inappropriate retention and will be unlikely to receive diplomas. Most in the field of special education would agree that keeping students with mental retardation back because they have not achieved grade-level work is absurd and serves no useful purpose. Indeed, such a practice is likely to be detrimental if these children lose contact with their age-appropriate peers. The larger issue is whether these children will "graduate" and receive some form of diploma that recognizes their accomplishment in school or drop out of school because they do not see the possibility of graduation. This is not an insignificant societal issue in that as many as 2 percent of children have some form of cognitive disability (U.S. Department of Education, 1996). Further, if these children receive high-quality services in school, they have a higher likelihood of being employed upon leaving school. Dropping out is associated with significantly poorer outcomes for all disabled students (Wagner et al., 1993). Therefore, setting standards policies without these children in mind may have a devastating impact on a relatively large number of students. Massachusetts has been grappling with this issue and has yet to reach a resolution.

A final point about high-stakes policy is that some aspects of the impact of these policies on students with disabilities are relevant for nondisabled students as well. There is relatively little support in the research for the use of high-stakes promotion policies as a vehicle for promoting higher achievement. In *High Stakes: Testing for Tracking, Promotion and Graduation*, Jay Heubert and Robert Hauser (1999) conclude, "The negative consequences, as grade retention is currently practiced, are that retained students persist in low achievement levels and are more likely to drop out of school" (p. 285). This finding also is consistent with the finding in the National Longitudinal Transition Study that failing high school subjects is associated with students with disabilities dropping out. In the remainder of this chapter, I discuss how educational policies and practices can be modified to assure that students with disabilities will benefit from standards-based reforms.

## INCREASING THE LIKELIHOOD THAT CHILDREN WITH DISABILITIES WILL PASS HIGH-STAKES TESTS

Though there are many unresolved issues and complications, in most states students with disabilities are part of some type of high-stakes testing program. Even in states that do not have high-stakes testing, academic outcomes need to be improved. Therefore, it is important to increase the likelihood that more students pass these tests and improve their academic performance. In addition to the recommendations in chapters 2, 3, and 4, the following recommendations should improve the likelihood that children will be able to achieve at higher levels and pass these tests.

### Start Early

As the research cited in the *Hancock* case indicates, appropriate early intervention for students experiencing reading and/or behavior difficulties in the primary grades increases the likelihood that students will perform better in school and decreases the likelihood that they will need special education services. Even for those who may ultimately need special education services due to a disability, the earlier students receive attention to these problems, the better.

As another example of universal design, it should also be noted that many students, both disabled and nondisabled, also need high-quality preschool services. Though children who have identified disabilities prior to enrollment in school are entitled to preschool services, most students who will ultimately be identified as needing special education services are not identified until after they enroll in school. Research on children who are at higher risk of reading difficulties in school, those from low-income environments or non-English-speaking environments, and those with disabilities has demonstrated that well-designed preschool programs can increase the likelihood of school success. Snow (1998) identified the characteristics of successful programs. These include close parent-program coordination; high language and literacy content, including rich opportunities to learn and practice these skills in motivating settings; and attention to phonemic awareness.

An important point to make here is that though high-quality preschool programs have been shown to be effective for both disabled and nondisabled children, many students who are identified as disabled students in school may not have benefited from these programs. First, most students with disabilities are identified after they start school, so the preschool entitlement of the IDEA is irrelevant to them. Further, many students who are at risk of being identified do not have access to preschool programs, or the ones to which they have access are of low quality (Snow, 1998). Therefore, given the evidence that suggests that those students with disabilities not passing are disproportionately poor, improving access to high-quality preschool programs for all students who are at risk of school difficulty has great promise.

## Curriculum Modification Should Be a Last Resort

In addition to having access to the general education curriculum consistent with the recommendations in chapter 3, educators and parents should be very conservative about modifications to the curriculum. It is increasingly apparent to me in my work in the schools that too many children with disabilities are receiving modified curriculum when accommodation would appear to be more appropriate. For example, it is completely appropriate to modify the reading curriculum for a child with dyslexia because that child cannot read at grade level. Her disability precludes her from doing so. However, her instruction in the rest of her subjects should be accommodated to address her access needs given her dyslexia. Too often this is not the case. For instance, she may receive a curriculum modification in a content area like science because she reads and writes below grade level. This practice could result in her not learning the same curriculum as her peers. The cumulative effect of this over years would likely result in her never passing the state science test. In some states that could mean that she would be denied a diploma. A far more appropriate response to her needs might be to provide her science book on tape and allow her to take her science tests on a computer on which she could access a spell-check feature. The IEP should be the vehicle by which this issue is forced.

In an age of accountability, special education directors, parents, and advocates should be deeply concerned with what appears to be a casual approach to modification and accommodation. In workshops I do with teachers, I find an alarming lack of understanding of the distinction between modifications and accommodations. Many use the two words interchangeably as if they were synonymous. It is therefore not surprising to see many IEPs of students with noncognitive disabilities with modifications in virtually every major subject area. Therefore, it is unlikely that these children will ever pass high-stakes tests. Being judicious about the use of modifications and encouraging the use of robust appropriate accommodations to achieve access to the curriculum are necessary conditions to improve the performance of students with disabilities on state and local assessments.

Further, the overmodification of curriculum can greatly hamper success in postsecondary settings. I recently gave a keynote address to the Association for Higher Education and Disability in which I brought up my concerns about the impact of modifications on educational attainment. I was greeted with enthusiastic applause. One university disability coordinator subsequently wrote to me expressing her concern over the lack of preparation of entering students with disability.

Many do not know that their high school programs were drastically modified. . . . In summary, students with disabilities are often: (a) very under-prepared in both knowledge and skills, (b) uninformed about special education modifications and resulting lack of preparations for the rigors of college, (c) unaware of the differences between high school and college and the implication of those differences for their college experiences, and (d) lack of self determination and independent living skills to succeed in college without special education and parental supports. (S. Vess, personal communication, August 11, 2004)

## Accommodations on Tests Should Mirror Instructional Accommodations

In addition to a conservative approach to modifications, educators and parents should carefully choose the accommodations a child receives. In general, accommodations should have a direct relationship to the impact of the child's disability and thus provide the child with a differential bounce in his performance (Fuchs & Fuchs, 1999). For instance, a child with dyslexia may need increased time to read material due to a slow reading rate. Without this accommodation the child would not be able to finish an assignment or a test, and thus his performance would be an underestimation of his ability to comprehend the content of a given text. Therefore, with the accommodation he would have a differential bounce compared with his nondisabled classmate who does not need extra time. It should also be noted that the wrong accommodation can depress performance of students with disabilities. For instance, extended time might be the wrong accommodation for a student with attentional issues if that student responds best to limits. But as the research of Katzman and others indicates, it appears that accommodations for children with disabilities may not be carefully chosen (Fuchs & Fuchs, 1999; Koretz & Hamilton, 2000). The students in Katzman's study had little knowledge of the accommodations they were receiving and the relationship of those accommodations to their disability. It appears that in some instances educators approach the decisions about accommodations as they do a menu, checking off what might be desirable without giving each item careful thought. This behavior is reinforced by many states and local districts that provide lists of "approved" accommodations.

Ultimately, a decision around accommodations should be an educational one and thus incorporated into the child's instructional program. Going back to the principle developed in chapter 2 concerning the goal of education as minimizing the impact of disability while maximizing opportunities to participate, decisions around accommodations are integral to that goal and thus should receive proper attention. For instance, using the example of the dyslexic again, the child with the laborious reading rate will need her entire educational program accommodated around this aspect of her disability. She may need both extra time on reading assignments and some content provided on audio tape. Her course selection should reflect the cumulative reading load of the courses. As Shaywitz (2003) writes, "For the dyslexic reader, accommodations represent the bridge that connects him to his strengths and, in the process, allows him to reach his potential. By themselves accommodations do not produce success; they are the catalyst for success. Accommodations grow in importance as a dyslexic progresses through schooling" (p. 314).

Thus, the issue is not just the accommodations students should receive during the high-stakes test but rather the important role well-thought-out accommodations play in the entire education process. The decisions concerning test accommodations should thus flow from instructional accommodations and be relatively straightforward. Waiting until test time to determine accommodations based on a list is indicative of a far greater problem in the child's total educational program.

In addition to the importance that accommodations play in the child's education and the measurement of his educational attainment level, accommodation decisions can provide the child with a deeper understanding of his own disability. This is important if the child is going to positively integrate his disability into his personality. Again, as advocated in chapter 2, children, particularly as they get older, need to understand the nature and impact of their disability if they are going to develop a positive outlook about their future. Involving students in discussions about their accommodations and the educational decisions that flow from them creates a great opportunity to develop this self-awareness. Further, as children move on to higher education and employment as adults, they will need this knowledge to help them become self-advocates.

### Time Devoted to Learning May Need to Be Lengthened

As the discussion on accommodations illustrates, time is an important accommodation for many students with disabilities. However, beyond giving students extra time to perform in certain instructional or testing situations, some students with disabilities may need extra time to learn important academic subjects. This is an important distinction. For instance, some students with disabilities have difficulty learning math concepts due to a number of reasons. A deaf student may not have learned the language needed to understand mathematical concepts. This may also be the case with a student who has an across-the-board language-based learning disability. It is not that these students cannot learn the concepts and associated operations and applications, it is just that they may need more instructional time. This can be a problem with many mathematics curricula that move at a very rapid pace. A recent piece of qualitative research of an inclusive mathematics program utilizing the Investigations curriculum that was conducted by a doctoral student at Harvard illustrated the problems many students with disabilities and their teachers face with fast-paced "constructivist" curriculum (Mutch-Jones, 2004). The students in this study had various disabilities, mostly learning disabilities and hearing impairments. They were taught in inclusive classrooms by both general and special education teachers, and the researcher focused on how these teachers delivered the curriculum. Of the many interesting findings of this study, the one that interested me most was the need teachers felt, particularly for the students with disabilities, to "loop back" to concepts taught earlier in order to teach new concepts. The teachers spoke of their frustration over not having enough time to work with students who were on the verge of getting important concepts. The failure of these students to master concepts had a cumulative effect on their mathematical development. When I read this study it became clear to me that the students simply needed more instructional time to learn these concepts, time that was not provided for in the design of the program.

A response that some districts use to address the issue of students who have not learned grade-level curricula is to retain them. This practice should be resisted. As stated previously, there is little evidence that retention works as a general policy, and there is considerable evidence that this practice is associated with dropping out of school (Heubert & Hauser, 1999). Retention should thus be avoided as a strategy to improve academic outcomes for students with disabilities.

The need for increasing instructional time to learn important subject matter must be addressed if we are going to improve academic performance and increase the number of students that pass high-stakes tests. For many students this may mean participating in extended school-year programs. The IDEA has required that in certain situations school districts must provide extended school-year programs in order to prevent regression and shorten the time needed to recoup skills lost during summer school vacations. In general, most school districts have provided these services to their most severely disabled populations. However, the demands brought about by standards-based reform should cause a reexamination of how and to whom extended school-year services are provided. For many students who simply require more time to learn important subject matter, extended school-year options may make all the difference. After-school programs may also be an effective option.

Another option that schools may consider is lengthening the time within the school day for certain subjects. Of course, such an approach involves trade-offs—other subject areas will receive less attention. Such trade-offs may make this option undesirable for many students. Extending the school day may thus be a preferred option for many students who need extra time to learn important concepts.

### Restructure High School Options through Effective Transition Planning

High school is the time high-stakes consequences are apt to have their most profound effect: the failure to graduate with a diploma. Thus, the use of instructional time spent in high school is central to assuring student success. Obviously, the students in Katzman's study who had not been taught geometry when they were tested in the tenth grade should have been taught geometry before they were tested. However, policy dictated that all children be tested at this grade. This is inappropriate in that the students are being given an early signal that they may not graduate. Though some might argue that this signal is appropriate because it might motivate them to work harder in school, the failure of these students to learn geometry was not their fault but rather that of the schools. This signal, coupled with its perceived injustice, may cause some of them to think more seriously about dropping out. This policy thus risks robbing these students of the "effort optimism" they will need to achieve the curriculum standards.

A more effective approach for these students would be to informally assess them relative to their acquisition of curriculum standards at the beginning of their high school career and develop their IEPs to assure opportunities to learn. This process must take a long view and help provide a road map that will span the high school years. This was the concept behind moving transition planning requirements from age 16 to age 14 in IDEA 1997. For some of the students in Katzman's study this process may have resulted in a decision that they receive three years of intensive math instruction before they take the MCAS to increase the likelihood that they will pass. Also, it may be necessary for some students to spend more than four years in high school or to participate in summer or after-school programs in order to meet the standards. It is important that students be directly involved in these decisions because they need to be aware of and take responsibility for the difficult work that may be required for them to meet the standards. However, as Katzman's research indicates, the students are motivated to stay in school and learn, and they understand the importance of standards. It is up to educators and parents to provide the opportunities that help ensure success.

# 6

# Policy

Over the past 30 years, the education of children with disabilities has drawn more federal oversight and regulation than any other area of K–12 education. Through the passage of Section 504 of the Rehabilitation Act and PL 94-142, now the Individuals with Disabilities Education Act (IDEA), Congress required that all children receive free and appropriate public education (FAPE) in the least restrictive environment (LRE) and backed up these regulations with strong due process protections. Over the years, Congress has extended the rights of children with disabilities to include early intervention and preschool services, as well as high school transition services. More recently, Congress has sought to include students with disabilities in school accountability systems through amendments to the IDEA in 1997 (IDEA 1997) and No Child Left Behind (NCLB). Policy, particularly federal policy, has an enormous influence on the education of these students and has been a major factor in improving the educational status of disabled students (Hehir & Gamm, 1999; President's Commission on Excellence in Special Education, 2002). Policy has thus evolved over the years from expanding educational opportunities for students with disabilities to a series of provisions designed to improve their educational outcomes. Understanding how policy at the federal level interacts with state and local policy is essential in guiding efforts to improve education for students with disabilities for a number of reasons.

First, laws are not self-implementing; they need to be enforced. Therefore, advocates can use their knowledge to leverage better education for students. A major role that policy and regulations serve in this area is specifying what can and cannot be done at the school level. For instance, current law prohibits ending educational services for students expelled from school. Knowledge of this requirement may help an advocate obtain services for a child who has been expelled.

Policy also can encourage certain innovations by permitting certain uses of funds or by providing grants for specific purposes. School innovators can use such funding for school improvement activities. For instance, the IDEA allows the use of federal special education funds to support "schoolwide" school improvement efforts under NCLB. Though a comprehensive discussion of all policies related to the education of students with disabilities is beyond the scope of this book, this chapter will focus on those areas of policy most relevant to improving educational results, eliminating ableism, and implementing universal design. For those seeking a deeper understanding of the law, I would recommend going to the website of the Council for Exceptional Children (www.ideapractices.org).

Some major policy issues relevant to the main concepts covered in this book include the participation of students with disabilities in standards-based accountability systems; the role of state and federal governments in supporting better educational opportunities; the discipline of students with disabilities; issues involving the development of individualized education programs (IEPs) and the reduction of paperwork; and "treatment-resistant" models of disability determination. Policies in these areas are in a state of flux, particularly as the 2004 reauthorization of the IDEA moves forward and regulations are finalized. This chapter, which presents an in-depth discussion of these issues, is organized around a set of policy positions that I believe will advance educational opportunities for students with disabilities. The following are important policy imperatives central to improving results for students with disability:

### 1. Support standards-based reform.

An important point to reiterate here is that the most damaging ableist assumption is the belief that disabled people are incapable. Therefore, the movement to include students with disabilities in standards-based reforms is promising and appears to be showing important results in some states (Ysseldyke et al., 2004). The standard for judging the efficacy of special education programs is rapidly moving from a process assessment (the implementation of procedural regulations) to one that includes outcome measures related to progress in the general education curriculum. The performance of students with disabilities on these tests is increasingly becoming a public issue that requires educators to examine their practices. Long-standing class-action litigations in Baltimore, Los Angeles, and the District of Columbia have been renegotiated with the parties involved to include requirements for the improved academic performance of students with disabilities (Sabel & Simon, 2004). The inclusion of students with disabilities in standards-based reform may be the most significant policy advance for these students since the passage of PL 94-142.

While it is true that standards-based reform is a promising policy development for students with disabilities, high-stakes testing that prevents students from being promoted or from receiving a diploma based on their performance on standardized tests is problematic. This is particularly true if we consider the concerns cited in the last chapter about basic access to the curriculum and about the construct validity of the tests. We run the risk of penalizing many children who have not had appropriate access to the curriculum.

Furthermore, many states are still working out the basic technical issues concerning accommodated testing for disabled students. Finally, some students may never be able to pass these tests due to the nature of their disability. No children with mental retardation will pass a high-content test. In a very real sense, some students with disabilities would have to become nondisabled in order to be promoted or graduate. This is ableism in the extreme. Thus, despite its promise, standards-based reform may ultimately reinforce current inequities if performance on high-stakes tests becomes the only means by which disabled students can demonstrate what they know and are able to do. It is important to note that disabled students are not the only group for whom high-stakes testing is being questioned (Heubert & Hauser, 1999). Other groups that have been poorly served by our educational systems, such as children from high-poverty backgrounds and children with limited English proficiency, may be equally harmed by these policies.

High-stakes consequences for students with disabilities may be an inappropriate policy at this time; nevertheless, school system accountability is crucial if standards-based reform is going to improve student performance. A central element of this accountability requires disaggregated data on the performance of disabled students on state assessments. Though this recommendation could be considered unnecessary due to NCLB's requirements to include children with disabilities in accountability systems, implementation of the law, and the U.S. Department of Education's (DOE) interpretation of it, shows that this issue is somewhat unsettled. A report in the *New York Times* on the implementation of the act raises some serious concerns:

> Many states have found ways to transform No Child Left Behind into something closer to Some Children Left Behind, particularly for disabled children and immigrants. More than a dozen states have adopted higher threshold numbers for counting these students in school ratings, so that they are frequently excluded from accountability systems. . . . In assessing schools, California and Texas include subgroups of 50 or more only if they account for 15

percent of the school's enrollment. Otherwise there must be 100 of them in California. In Texas, there must be 200. (Schemo, 2004)

The inclusion of subgroups such as disabled students in school-level accountability systems does raise legitimate concerns. For instance, at the elementary level in Massachusetts, students are assessed under MCAS (a state assessment tool) only in grade four. In a small elementary school with only two fourth-grade classes, that may mean only four or five students with disabilities are tested annually. Making assertions about the efficacy of school programs based on such small numbers is likely to be invalid. Many school officials are advocating to remove subgroups from school-level accountability within the NCLB framework that potentially involves significant sanctions at the school level. This is understandable and in many cases legitimate.

Another unintended consequence of including students with disabilities in school-level accountability systems in which the school can experience sanctions may be that schools avoid enrolling students likely to do poorly on these tests. I have been working with a small inclusive elementary school in Boston that has done very well over the past few years in student performance, receiving many local and national awards. This past year the school has been cited for failure to achieve "adequate yearly progress" due to a decline in fourth-grade MCAS scores. When the principal investigated, she found that four students were largely responsible for the decline, and of these, three transferred into the school from other schools. Only one student had been enrolled in the school since kindergarten, and that student had fairly significant disabilities. The principal was concerned that landing on a "watch list" had demoralized her staff and led them to question the school's open enrollment. This school is very popular with parents of disabled students due to its inclusive philosophy and strong results. Thus, the inclusion of students with disabilities in school-level accountability systems may have perverse results in some circumstances.

Despite the problems associated with including students with disabilities in school-level accountability systems, particularly in small schools, it is important to disaggregate performance and hold school districts accountable. The question is the unit(s) of accountability. In larger schools, an element of school-level responsibility is more reasonable. In smaller schools, accountability for results over several years may be a more desirable and valid measure of program efficacy. However, there should always be a significant level of school-level accountability so that those closest to the child will be motivated to improve educational opportunities. An article in the *Boston Globe* (Schworm, 2004b) underscores the importance of disaggregating data for students with disabilities. Because Massachusetts requires disaggregated reporting and accountability measures, many previously high-performing, affluent schools are landing on the state's "in need of improvement" list. The copresident of an affluent school's parent organization said this confirmed her fears that pockets of students were not fulfilling their potential. Former U.S. secretary of education Rod Paige is quoted in the *Globe* article: "We're not saying it's a bad school . . . but when we measure the aggregate it hides a lot of failure." The piece ends with a comment from the district's director of special education, Linda Croteau: "Schools like us are going to be in the forefront of answering the question of how do we help these harder-to-reach kids." This attention to the performance of disabled students is a far cry from the lack of accountability for educational results that has long plagued special education, and it is cause for optimism in terms of improving educational opportunity.

Although attention to educational performance is hopeful, change will require concerted effort. Therefore, school accountability systems should include a significant element of shared responsibility between the district and the school. This is particularly true in special education, where a school district's policies and practices can have a great influence on building-level results. For instance, some school districts "cluster" large numbers of students with disabilities in certain schools, which can result in fewer opportunities for inclusionary placements due to the disproportionately large numbers of disabled students in a given school. Furthermore, the large number of students at one site may distort scores, depending on the type of disabilities the students have. Teacher assignments may also have an impact on student performance. Many districts have difficulty recruiting qualified special education teachers and thus may assign a disproportionate number of unqualified teachers to certain schools. A shared accountability system is therefore more likely to result in meaningful change.

### 2. *Hold states accountable for improving educational results for students with disabilities.*

Under a shared accountability system, states too must be held accountable for the performance of disabled students. States can have a major influence on the educational opportunities available to children. For instance, as the *Hancock* case illustrates, holding districts or individual schools solely accountable for performance when they have not received the resources they need to meet high academic standards is unfair and not likely to result in significant improvement. As the court ruled, Massachusetts should be held accountable for its failure to adequately fund schools in poor communities. It should also be emphasized that the IDEA is a state-grant program, which means that states are primarily accountable for implementing the act. Other areas in which states should be held accountable include teacher preparation, curriculum development, civil rights enforcement, and interagency collaboration. IDEA 2004 has important new provisions that are designed to increase state-level accountability. They will be discussed later in this chapter.

*Teacher Preparation*   Local districts with few qualified special education teachers are at a distinct disadvantage in their efforts to improve educational results and provide for the needs of their disabled students. For instance, the Los Angeles Unified School District (LAUSD) has had to employ significant numbers of uncertified special education teachers. In 2004, only 70.6 percent of special education teachers were certified, and the district experienced major difficulty in hiring speech pathologists (Trent, 2004). Not only has this had a negative impact on students, but it has become a legal issue for the district. The district has responded by recruiting extensively and developing its own training programs. This situation takes on greater legal consequence under IDEA 2004, which aligns with "highly qualified" provisions of NCLB. Broadly interpreted, this means that teachers must be qualified to teach the subjects they are teaching. IDEA 2004 also adds the requirement that special education teachers be qualified to teach core subjects in accordance with NCLB (Section 602 [10] A, C–F). Clearly, the LAUSD and many other local education agencies (LEAs) cannot meet this requirement on their own. California and other states will have to enhance their efforts to recruit qualified providers.

*Curriculum Development*   Many states have been developing state curricula frameworks that are aligned with their accountability systems. States that have clearly defined standards as to what students should know and be able to do and assessment programs that measure their attainment are more likely to increase student performance. Here again, the Massachusetts experience is illustrative. Massachusetts has engaged in a decade-long process of defining these frameworks, training teachers on them, and aligning state curriculum frameworks with the MCAS. This may have contributed to the state's improved performance on national indicators.

*Interagency Collaboration*   Another area where state activity is crucial is in serving the role of interagency collaboration. This role is particularly critical in special education, where a child's success may depend on whether he or she receives services from multiple state agencies. For instance, children with significant emotional disturbance may need mental health services, home supports, and community programs in order to increase their chances of success within their families and their communities. Educators and mental health professionals increasingly recognize that success for these children cannot be accomplished by schools alone. As discussed in chapter 4, a movement called systems of care, which has been spreading across the country, seeks to "wrap services around" children with mental health needs and their families. Such efforts can be greatly enhanced through state initiatives, and, if successful, they can help support improved educational performance for many students with disabilities. Other children with disabilities and their families, such as those needing medical supports or home supports, require interagency supports as well. For instance, a family that needs a home health aide whose services are not paid for by the family's health insurance may need a Medicaid income waiver in order to receive this type of support.

Given the goal of minimizing disability and maximizing the ability of children to participate in their community, well-functioning interagency programs are crucial. The converse is also true: When state agencies fail to work together to support children and families, some parents may be forced to institutionalize, hospitalize, or place their children in residential schools, thus accentuating the impact of their children's disabilities and restricting their ability to participate. Other parents may be forced to give up employment, thus affecting the whole family's prospects.

The state's role in interagency collaboration is so important to school administrators and parents that both groups supported amendments to the IDEA in 1997 that require states to oversee this activity. This requirement, which was reaffirmed in IDEA 2004, requires the chief executive officer of a state to have mechanisms in place to ensure the coordination of services across state agencies. Further, the law prohibits state agencies from denying any services to a child that they would normally provide using the excuse that that child is also served under the IDEA (IDEA 2004, Section 612 [2] A). This is an important protection for school districts that have complained that some state agencies were refusing to fund services for children covered under the IDEA. Advocates, parents, and school personnel who want to promote the well-being of children and families in their state should become aware of their state's efforts in this area and use this provision of the law to leverage change.

*Civil Rights Enforcement*   Finally, an important area of state-level activity relevant to improving results for students with disabilities concerns civil rights enforcement. The rights of students with disabilities to appropriate accommodations, supports, and services is a matter of law that states are responsible for ensuring under the IDEA's requirements of "general supervision under the act" (IDEA 2004, Section 612 [11]). The requirements that flow from this section of the act are rather comprehensive and require assurance that the requirements of Part B of the act, the state grant program out of which most regulatory requirements affecting the education of children with disabilities flow, have been met. Importantly, a state is responsible for determining whether its LEAs are eligible to receive special education funds, based on the assumption that the LEA is in compliance with the law. The Office of Special Education Programs (OSEP) of the U.S. Department of Education has historically required that states have internal monitoring systems to meet this requirement.

However, in reality, few states serve this role effectively (Hehir, 2002; National Council on Disability, 1996, 2001). Although due process complaint systems can be highly effective in ensuring that students with disabilities have their needs met, relatively few parents use these systems, and most that do tend to be affluent, as the exercise of these rights often requires hiring a lawyer (Hehir, 1990). Therefore, states need to take on an enforcement role for the vast majority of students. While many in schools view compliance monitoring as somehow removed from educational results (Hehir, 1990), the importance of students receiving the accommodations, supports, and services they need is directly tied to student outcomes. And, as the *Hancock* case indicates, poorer students are less likely to get what they need without state intervention and support.

It should also be noted that although a state's internal monitoring may be weak, some states have been defendants in major class-action suits involving implementation of the IDEA at the local level. Notable among these is *Corey H. et al. v. City of Chicago et al.* in which the district was found to be incompliant with the least restrictive environment requirements of this case. The judge found that the state of Illinois failed to meet its duties under the general supervision provisions of the IDEA:

> Children with disabilities in the Chicago public schools have been and continue to be segregated into separate and unequal educational environments, contrary to established federal law. Although the local school district has recognized its deficiencies and agreed to a remedial plan, the State educational agency has continued to deny its responsibilities. The denial conflicts with clear Congressional intent to make the State ultimately responsible for compliance with longstanding federal mandate that children with disabilities be educated in the least restrictive environment. (cited in Hehir & Gamm, 1999, p. 226)

The logical question about the importance of the states' role concerns to whom states are accountable. Of course, state education departments are responsible to their legislatures and their governors, and major progress can and does occur through these channels. The Massachusetts school reform initiatives, for example, have been largely state driven. Disability activists have also been effective in promoting reform through state-level activity. For instance, advocates in California were successful in getting a law through the state legislature, the Hughes Bill, which required "positive behavioral supports" for students with disabilities. Also, as in *Hancock*, courts can hold states accountable. However, relying solely on the courts is inappropriate and inefficient. Therefore, both the IDEA and NCLB envision a significant federal role in ensuring state-level accountability.

A shared system of accountability, however, should not let the federal government off the hook. States should be able to look to the federal government for support, and the country has a right to expect the federal government to hold states accountable for their responsibilities as defined in federal law. In turn, states should be able to expect sufficient federal funding to support meeting the requirements of NCLB and the IDEA. Furthermore, the federal government has an ongoing role in supporting research and technical assistance relevant to state and local efforts to improve education results. Congress requires that the federal government monitor state implementation of grant programs and civil rights legislation: Both NCLB and the IDEA require states to meet various conditions in order to receive federal funds, and the civil rights of students with disabilities are monitored by the Office of Civil Rights under Section 504 of the Rehabilitation Act. The available evidence would suggest that the federal government could improve its performance in all these areas.

### 3. Improve federal monitoring.

Though the federal government's responsibility for monitoring the IDEA is well established in the law, its role traditionally has been relatively weak. The number of federal employees devoted to this function is very small, only about 50. Both Congress and previous administrations have resisted assertive enforcement (Hehir, 2002). Thus, it is not surprising that OSEP has been widely criticized by advocates for not appropriately monitoring special education. The National Council on Disability conducted a study in 1996 on federal monitoring and found that

> despite progress in the last decade in educating students with disabilities, current federal and state laws have failed to ensure the delivery of a free appropriate public education for too many students with disabilities. . . . Lack of accountability, poor enforcement, and systemic barriers have robbed too many students of their educational rights and opportunities and have produced a separate system of education for students with disabilities rather than one unified system that ensures full and equal physical, programmatic, and communication access for all students.

The federal government's failure to monitor special education more effectively is likely due to a complex set of political factors (Hehir, 2002). Given that the major enforcement mechanism has been to withhold state funds, federal officials' reluctance to use this remedy may be understandable. However, failure in this area often means that parents and advocates are forced to turn to due process hearings or the courts to seek enforcement of their children's rights. Therefore, because relatively few have the means to seek this form of redress, the needs of many students go unmet.

In IDEA 1997, Congress gave the Department of Education more flexible enforcement options, including partial withholding. These provisions were revised and strengthened in IDEA 2004, under which states must produce a state performance plan that will play a central role in the federal monitoring of each state. The statute is quite specific in detailing enforcement mechanisms available to the secretary of education, such as interventions and withholding funds. The new law also clearly says that the states must monitor LEAs (IDEA 2004, Section 616).

These new mechanisms, coupled with a more focused, data-based federal monitoring system, could help promote better educational results for students with disabilities. In addition to a greater commitment of staff resources, the Department of Education will be required to revise its monitoring system to be a more outcomes-based, data-driven system (IDEA 2004, Section 616). The monitoring of outcome measures must be used to determine the status of a state's eligibility to receive funds under the act. Areas in which such goals could be established based on current data include participation rates in statewide testing, the degree to which children are educated in general education classes, dropout rates, graduation rates, and rates of minority placement in special education. Incorporating outcome standards in the monitoring could move the nation toward a more uniform implementation of the act and away from the current process orientation.

### 4. Increase federal funding for special education and NCLB.

Both the IDEA and NCLB are woefully underfunded, which appears to have an impact on results. As the *Hancock* case illustrates, the availability of special education funding can influence outcomes. Congress has been widely criticized for not funding the IDEA at the 40 percent authorization level. The call to increase federal support for the IDEA has been growing in Congress as school districts and parents seek a greater funding role for Washington. During the 2003–04 school year, the federal government funded approximately 18 percent of the excess cost of providing special education (National Association of State Boards of Education, 2004). Some view this law as an unfunded mandate, and although this is not technically true, since the IDEA is a voluntary state grant program, the perception is strong. Advocates for a greater level of federal funding also use the law's original commitment of up to 40 percent of excess cost to reinforce the notion that the federal government has been derelict in its responsibilities to fund the program (IDEA 2004, Section 611).

Although achieving the promised 40 percent has gained some momentum, the reality of federal funding priorities makes this a daunting goal. The additional amount of money required approaches $15 billion (IDEA 2004, Section 611). In IDEA 2004, Congress authorized amounts that will reach the 40 percent goal by 2011 (IDEA 2004, Section 611). However, it is important to reiterate that authorized funds are not appropriated funds and that Congress annually appropriates funds for state grant programs. Therefore, there is no promise that these funds will ever materialize. For instance, the president's request for funds for fiscal year 2006 is approximately $11 billion, even though IDEA 2004 authorizes over $14.5 billion.

Obviously, the administration and many in Congress are, therefore, not committed to reaching this level of funding. Furthermore, some members of Congress express reluctance to increase funding significantly due to concerns about the program. At a hearing at which I testified about the placement of large numbers of minority students in special education, one member expressed his reluctance to increase funding, stating, "This is good money chasing bad."

Even though reaching the 40 percent level may not be realistic at this time, Congress should not be off the hook for providing more resources. A way to support increased appropriations while not subsidizing questionable practices might be to target increases for specific purposes. One possibility would be to subsidize school districts for the cost of educating students with significant disabilities. These children, depending on how we define them, represent a subset of children served under the act who have significant, usually medically based disabilities that result in needs that often require school districts to incur costs several times those for nondisabled students. I would define this group as students with low-incidence disabilities, ones that occur in less than one half of 1 percent of the population (moderate to severe mental retardation, blindness, deafness, etc.). These children together represent approximately 20 percent of the students served under the IDEA, or approximately 2 percent of all students in K–12. Further, these conditions exist in relatively constant numbers across populations, with a slightly higher incidence in high-poverty populations (Hehir & Gamm, 1999). Congress could target increases through annual appropriations bills to subsidize the education of these students using a census and poverty-weighted formula. An advantage of this approach is that it targets money where it is most needed and to a population whose eligibility for services is beyond dispute.

Another option that Congress could consider through the annual appropriations process that could greatly help states improve results would be to target money to low-income districts for specific purposes. A particularly productive use of such funds might be to provide early intervention for students experiencing reading and behavior difficulties. Given that these services should be part of general education, the funding for these services may more appropriately come through NCLB rather than from special education. Research has consistently shown that providing intervention for students experiencing early problems in learning to read or to behave appropriately in school can reduce the number of students requiring special education. Furthermore, the current practice of intervening late, typically in fourth or fifth grade, for students with learning or behavioral disabilities is less than effective. Targeting the money to these research-based approaches in K–3 would both help disabled students and result in fewer inappropriate referrals. The White House has advocated this approach, and a paper written by former Bush presidential advisor Reid Lyon and several colleagues entitled "Rethinking Learning Disabilities" describes this approach in detail. It is important to reemphasize that these programs should be regular education interventions: "A label is not necessary for implementation of prevention programs, and the cost of delaying is too great to wait" (Lyon et al., 2001, p. 277).

### 5. Design universal discipline policies for all students.

The issue of discipline and students with disabilities is a long-standing and contentious issue. The basic issue at hand has revolved around two questions. The first is the degree to which we can hold students accountable for behavior that arises out of their disability—essentially, behavior they cannot control. The other has to do with the obligation school districts have concerning the provision of services for students who have been suspended for a long term from school or expelled. IDEA 1997 included significant revisions of the law in this area that were designed to clarify these issues while giving school districts increased flexibility in disciplining students with disabilities. These provisions were a result of compromises between disability advocates and school interests and had their basis in a 1994 dispute between the Department of Education and the state of Virginia.

In 1994, the DOE was informed by advocates in Virginia that the state was not providing services for students with disabilities who had been expelled from school for behavior not considered a manifestation of their disability. (See IDEA 1997 for the definition of manifestation and for the legal requirements for determination.) The DOE informed Virginia that if it would not assure that these students would receive free and appropriate public education, the department would withhold its IDEA grant. A period of intense negotiation and political opposition ensued. Though the DOE assured Virginia's chief state school officer that the state could legally expel students as long as it continued to provide services, Virginia refused to serve these students. Republican governor George Allen publicly criticized the Clinton administration's action as being soft on school discipline. I recall getting a call from the DOE's deputy chief of staff, who had been informed by the White House that the president had read the governor's criticism in the press clips and wanted to know what the DOE was doing. She warned me, "You're going to have to explain this one, Tom." As we had done with Secretary Richard Riley prior to the enforcement action, we explained to the White House that we were enforcing the first Bush administration's interpretation that, under the IDEA, all students were entitled to FAPE, even those expelled from school. We explained further that this interpretation was central to the statute's requirement that "all students" meant all students, a principle that was reinforced by a U.S. Supreme Court decision, *Timothy R. v. Rochester, New Hampshire*. The White House supported our action, even though it was politically risky to do so. I received another call from Virginia's Democratic senator, Chuck Robb, who implored us to seek a compromise.

The disability advocacy community strongly supported the administration's action. The committee saw Virginia as undermining the fundamental principle of the IDEA, that all disabled students were entitled to FAPE, and that any compromise of that principle could bring about more widespread exclusion. In a meeting shortly after the action, disability community leaders unanimously urged Secretary Riley to hold firm on the issue. Governor Allen was equally adamant and continued to publicly criticize the administration's action as an overreach of federal authority that was undermining school safety. An example of the irreconcilable positions taken by the governor and the disability community on this issue was evident in a televised debate Allen had with a parent advocate, Stephanie Lee. (Lee became director of OSEP during the current Bush administration.) The mother of a young woman with Down's syndrome, Lee had worked on Capitol Hill for the Republicans. Though her daughter was well behaved and not at risk of being expelled, Lee, like other disability advocates, saw Allen's action as a threat to the fundamental principles of the IDEA. Lee strongly supported the DOE position in her first television appearance. Her support, along with that of other Republican disability advocates, laid the political foundation for the battles that would ensue over the reauthorization of the IDEA. They represented strong bipartisan opposition to any weakening of the act.

Virginia ultimately brought suit against the DOE's action in the Fourth Circuit Court and won. The court agreed with Virginia that the DOE's interpretation of the statute was faulty and that the IDEA did not contain language that protected students expelled from school. However, Virginia's victory was temporary. When the IDEA was reauthorized in 1997, both the Clinton administration and the disability community insisted that the "Virginia problem" be corrected statutorily by insisting upon language that prohibited cessation of services for students expelled from school. This was not an easy sell, but both parties held firm. I recall an incident when the administration sent up a statement of position (SOP) on a draft version of the IDEA that did not include the sought-after language. A draft of the SOP that Assistant Secretary Judy Heumann and I were reviewing did not address the issue either. Kay Cassteavens, assistant secretary for legislation, met with us and said that we were not going to prevail on this matter. She suggested that the only way it could be saved was for Judy to meet personally with the president's senior staff. That day, Judy wheeled (she uses a wheelchair) up to the White House with Kay and met with the president's senior staff, and we did prevail. Kay informed me afterward that Judy had won the issue single-handedly. Her argument that the disability community was solidly behind this position was undoubtedly not lost on the White House political operatives. (See Shapiro, 1994, for a discussion of the political strength of the disability community.) As a result, IDEA 1997 included strong language prohibiting the cessation of services for students with disabilities who were suspended or expelled from school.

However, the issue of discipline was not resolved in 1997 and was addressed again in IDEA 2004. Among other things, the bill continues to provide significant protections in the area of discipline while at the same time giving school districts greater flexibility in removing students who exhibit disciplinary problems. The bill also provides clearer language regarding manifestation determinations. Importantly, the new law does continue to require that services be provided to all students with disabilities who are suspended or expelled from school for more than ten days, but it also allows the removal of students with disabilities from existing placements for behavior if it is not a manifestation of a disability. The law defines manifestation narrowly as being "caused by" or having a "direct substantial relationship" to the child's disability or as being due to the "direct result" of the LEA's failure to implement the IEP. The law protects from removal the child whose behavior is determined to be a manifestation of disability, except under what the law defines as special circumstances, such as weapon or drug possession or if the child inflicts serious bodily injury on another at school (IDEA 2004, Section 615 [K]). Though Congress may permit easier removal, schools are not required to remove children for whom such removal may not be in the child's best interest. School districts are free to go beyond the IDEA in serving children as long as that service does not violate the act. As my former law professor Jay Heubert once stated, "Just because something is legal doesn't make it right."

One of the main controversies surrounding the education of disabled students is the imposition of a "double standard" concerning their discipline. That is, the protections under the IDEA can mean that students who are guilty of the same infraction may have different consequences applied. Although there may be some justification for this differential treatment of students whose disabilities prevent them from controlling their behavior, applying a different standard for other students with disabilities who willfully break school rules could undermine school discipline policies. For instance, in many districts a child who assaults a teacher will be expelled from school. Under existing federal law, if the expelled child has a disability, he or she is entitled to continuing educational services, while the nondisabled child may not be.

Many school administrators claim that this gives a mixed message to students. I agree with this view. Holding students with disabilities to a different standard when they knowingly break rules by behaving in a way that is not a manifestation of their disability is a bad practice. The message in a sense is ableist and patronizing in that it implies that disabled students cannot abide by rules. Further, such practices may set a disabled student up for future failure if he or she does not learn the importance of developing appropriate social behavior in school. The question becomes whether it is possible to design school discipline programs that protect the legitimate rights of the minority of disabled students whose disability necessitates some differential in discipline procedures while appropriately holding most disabled students accountable for their behavior. I believe the answer is yes.

First, for the small number of students whose behavior is a manifestation of their disability, the rigid application of school rules by punishing these students for some of these behaviors may not make sense and is illegal. Though these behaviors generally should not be ignored, the goal with these students should be to develop behaviors that are more socially acceptable. This generally requires significant work with well-thought-out behavioral interventions that are consistently applied. These approaches may have to involve other students as well. I was in a school that had successfully included a fifth grader with significant autism. Having observed the child for a full day, I was impressed with how both the staff and students supported him. In a meeting with a couple of his classmates, I asked how they responded when John had a behavior problem. A pensive classmate responded, "Specifically which behavior are you referring to?" To me this response spoke volumes. The school had done a great job in coordinating its behavior support efforts for John. But the classmate's response also showed that children are capable of understanding the need to respond to the behavior of some significantly disabled students differently. This is important, in that children need to understand why discipline rules might have to be applied differently in some instances if they are going to view school discipline procedures as fair and just. I believe the students in this school would have considered it unfair and absurd if John was punished the same way for every rule infraction as his classmates.

The majority of disabled students can and should live by school rules. However, as the discussion about the Virginia case illustrates, disability advocates most fear the separation of disabled students from school through long-term suspensions or expulsions. This fear is justified. First, disabled students already have much higher dropout rates, and dropping out is associated with very bad outcomes for disabled students: an increased likelihood of problems with the law, unemployment, and early teenage pregnancies (Wagner et al., 1993). A pattern of frequent suspensions and expulsions from school can predispose students to dropping out. In addition, disabled students who drop out have fewer options than their nondisabled counterparts. Some may find it more difficult to access alternative programs designed for dropouts, such as GED programs, given the educational deficits more common among disabled students.

Obviously, frequent suspension from school is likely to cause educational deficits for nondisabled students as well. Thus, federal law should be "universally designed" to incorporate the principle of prohibiting the cessation of services for all students, ideally through an amendment to NCLB. Special education law rightly recognizes that expulsions or long-term suspensions without services almost always prevent acceptable progress in school and increase the likelihood that a child will drop out of school (Wagner et al., 1993). The same is likely true for nondisabled children. Children who are not in school are less likely to be able to meet higher standards. An analysis of attendance records of students in Massachusetts reveals a significant correlation between MCAS failure and frequent absences from school. Consequently, the Massachusetts Department of Education currently factors in school attendance in its monitoring of adequate yearly progress under NCLB.

Consistent with this approach, a clear standard should be established to determine at what point a series of suspensions represents functional exclusion and therefore triggers the requirement for continued educational services. Clearly, providing educational services for a student who might be suspended for a day or two is impractical, and IDEA regulations recognize the need for considerable flexibility here. The law's requirements for providing continuing educational services do not kick in until after ten days of suspension, or when a series of suspensions over time amounts to cessation of services (IDEA 2004). The vagueness and complexity of special education regulations and the double standard they create could be solved by establishing a clear policy for all children that requires the continuation of educational services when cumulative suspensions reach ten days.

Given a system universally designed in the manner described above, much of the current regulations in this area can be streamlined and revised in a manner that can be easily understood.

### 6. Reduce paperwork and improve IEPS.

One reason many teachers leave special education is that they feel buried in paperwork (Coleman, 2000). Clearly, we need to make sure we have sufficient numbers of qualified personnel to serve students with disabilities. (The issue of special education teacher preparation is addressed more extensively in chapter 3.) If we are going to improve educational results, we need to assure that the teachers we have spend as much time as possible working with children, families, and other professionals.

Many providers look to the IEP as the place to reduce paperwork. School staff refer to thick IEPs with extensive goals and objectives. However, many parents view IEPs as the heart of the law, the vehicle by which their children receive free and appropriate education in the least restrictive environment. Further, many parents of children with disabilities view calls for paperwork reduction as a thinly veiled attempt to reduce their children's rights or an effort by the school district to avoid accountability. Some counter that much of the paperwork burden is the result of requirements added by local school districts and states, some of which are designed to curb costs or increase the likelihood that districts will prevail in due process hearings. Are these irreconcilable positions? I do not think so. I believe that there is significantly more common ground on this issue than might appear at first glance.

Both parents and school staff have a deep interest in making sure that there are sufficient qualified providers to work with their children. Many parents also complain about excessive paperwork. I remember a meeting I had with a colleague who was also the parent of a young man with disabilities. She had two file drawers full of paperwork concerning her son, who at the time had just graduated from high school. I recall her saying that most of it wasn't worth the paper it was printed on. She told me that even with all the forms and evaluations, her son's school district fought her for years as she worked to get him included. She said that what was important to her was that her son be taught the same subjects as the other students. She finally achieved her goal when he was in high school and told me that it has made all the difference, now that he is fully integrated into his community as an adult.

IDEA 2004 makes some changes related to IEP content that are aimed at reducing paperwork. Specifically, the law requires short-term objectives only for students participating in the alternative assessment program, generally a relatively small number of students with cognitive disabilities (IDEA 2004, Section 614 [D]). This change should help reduce paperwork for providers. Another potentially important change in IDEA 2004 allows the establishment of up to 15 pilot demonstration proposals that will allow for the development of multiyear IEPs. This pilot program has significant restrictions and requires the secretary to report annually to Congress on the effectiveness of these demonstrations (IDEA 2004, Section 614 [E]).

Though these changes may reduce paperwork, it is important to make sure that changing the format of IEPs also improves education for children, particularly in the context of NCLB. Given the centrality of the IEP to special education, I believe this is an optimal time for school staff and parents to revise this IEP process and content. It is time for parents and schools to come together around a common set of interests, improving education for disabled students. The common ground lies in embracing the intent of the law concerning IEPs as the driver of improved education for students with disabilities. Parents want education based on high expectations for their children, and they want educators to be accountable for meeting their children's needs. In short, they want the IEP to drive appropriate education and successful outcomes for their children. Educators should want the same thing.

As should be clear from the discussion in chapter 5, the landscape has changed significantly in special education with the passage of the 1997 amendments and more recently with No Child Left Behind. We can no longer be content to simply implement procedures and provide services. We are increasingly responsible for educational results. Like parents, educators should view the IEP as driving change and accountability.

We should be seeking more powerful IEPs that are tightly focused on gaining access to the curriculum and meeting the unique needs that arise out of each child's disability. IEPs that go on for pages, listing goals and objectives that are disconnected from the curriculum, do not meet this standard. On the other hand, an IEP for a child with dyslexia that specifically addresses how that child will be taught to read and write, how that child will participate in state-level assessments, and how that child will gain access to other subjects is an IEP that parents and school administrators should embrace. For instance, the IEP should have goals specified only in areas in which the curriculum is being modified for a student with disabilities or when the IEP addresses unique needs that arise out of the child's disability, such as the need to learn Braille. In areas where accommodations or supports are needed, the IEP should simply state the nature of these requirements. And, depending on the child's disability, these accommodations may be constant from year to year. In short, IEPs should be designed to minimize the impact of disability and maximize the ability of children to participate in school and their community.

For example, an IEP for a child with dyslexia would focus specifically on how that child will be taught to read and write. This goes directly to the needs that arise out of the child's disability. Goals and benchmarks should be developed. However, for the rest of the curriculum, the IEP should address how the child will access the curriculum given her dyslexia; that is, the accommodations and supports that child will receive. There would be no need for additional goals and benchmarks, because for every subject except language arts the child's goals should be the grade-appropriate curriculum goals. The child's assessment accommodations should mirror her instructional accommodations, which may apply across curriculum areas and may be the same or similar from year to year. The annual reviews would thus focus directly on the impact of the child's disability and would be a time to fine-tune the child's program based on the program's success. Therefore, a well-constructed IEP would not require lots of additional paperwork. This is the type of IEP that both parents and school administrators should embrace and that would be a huge step forward compared to many IEPs.

Though this change may be significant in practice, it comports with the law in both substance and spirit. Simply put, IEPs would specify that goals and benchmarks should only be required when addressing the unique needs that arise out of a child's disability and only in areas where the child is receiving modified, non-age-appropriate curriculum. Thus, the length and specificity of the IEP would be a function of the impact of the disability. Under this standard, a student with significant cognitive disabilities might have a much more involved IEP because he would need to have more areas of the curriculum modified, and he may have other specific needs rising out of his disability. However, it should be noted that most children with disabilities have a high-incidence, noncognitive disability and thus should not be receiving most of their subjects in a modified form. Therefore, the reduction in paperwork that would result from this proposal would be considerable.

The issue of paperwork reduction should not boil down to whether we require short-term objectives or seek multiyear IEPs but to making the IEP process and product more meaningful to both parents and educators while eliminating unnecessary paperwork for both. However, beyond paperwork reduction, this proposal should be embraced because it will call attention to what is potentially a bad practice, as cited in the previous chapter: the inappropriate modification of curriculum for students with disabilities. In the above example it is completely appropriate to modify the reading curriculum for a child with dyslexia because that child can't read at grade level. Her disability precludes her from doing so. However, her instruction in the rest of her subjects should be accommodated to address her access needs, given her dyslexia. If, for instance, her science curriculum was modified because she reads and writes below grade level, she would not be learning the same curriculum as her peers, and the cumulative effect of this over the years would likely preclude her from ever passing the state science test. In some states that could mean she would be denied a diploma. A far more appropriate response to her needs might be to provide her with a science book on tape and allow her to take her science tests on a computer where she could access a spell-check. The IEP should be the vehicle to force this issue. Being judicious about the use of modifications and encouraging the use of robust appropriate accommodations to gain access to the curriculum are necessary conditions to improve the performance of students with disabilities on state and local assessments.

### 7. Increase funding for research and support programs.
The discretionary programs funded under the IDEA are designed to improve implementation of the IDEA through research, technical assistance, technology development, teacher preparation,

and parent training. Special education is a large enterprise serving a highly diverse population, and Part D of the IDEA is its research and development (R&D) arm. All of these functions take on greater importance within a results-oriented framework. The field needs high-quality research and technical assistance to improve educational results for students with disabilities. Examples of research needs include such diverse topics as the best approaches to prepare preschoolers with disabilities to be successful in school; the optimum approach to teaching English to children whose primary language is American Sign Language; the most effective behavioral interventions for students with autism; and the most appropriate uses of communication devices for students who are nonverbal. Given the fact that the IDEA covers 13 disability areas from birth to early adulthood, the list of unmet research needs is extensive. Also, the need to get research into the hands of teachers, school administrators, and parents is crucial.

Although the federal government has supported significant research and innovation in the field, the appropriation levels for these activities have been very inadequate. Only about $340 million was appropriated for all discretionary programs under the IDEA in federal fiscal year 2005, and only $83 million of that amount is for research (see the Council for Exceptional Children website at www. ideapractices.org), or less than 1 percent of the annual amount the country spends on special education. The inadequacy of this commitment was brought home to me when OSEP sponsored a research conference at Gallaudet University several years ago, bringing together the top researchers in deafness from across the country to establish a research agenda. The unmet research needs the group identified exceeded the whole research budget for all of special education. Yet deaf children represent a small percentage of the students served by the IDEA (U.S. Department of Education, 2003). All of the identified research needs were legitimate, given the very low educational attainment level of large numbers of deaf students; many high school students function at the fourth- or fifth-grade level. Most needs will remain unaddressed unless the federal government increases its appropriation; there is no other source of significant research support in this area.

No major business could prosper with so little money devoted to R&D. Given the significant national commitment to special education, it is important that this money be wisely spent on research-validated practices. Unless the federal government invests in R&D, the likelihood that money will be spent inefficiently is great. A way to address this issue would be for Part D of the IDEA to be funded as a percentage of the Part B grant. This could be based on a constant percentage of the 40 percent federal commitment. If this level were set at 10 percent of the federal Part B state grant program, this would yield a 4 percent commitment of total national effort devoted to R&D. Sufficient funding would vastly increase knowledge development and utilization and would provide a predictable funding source that would enable multiyear planning and commitments. Such an effort could greatly improve educational results for students with disabilities.

### 8. Provide increased support for the preparation of personnel in special education and related services.

The federal government has supported the preparation of personnel for special education and related services for three decades under the IDEA and its predecessor, PL 89-313. This support has helped prepare teachers, teacher educators, researchers, and administrators in special education. These funds have also been used to promote innovation in higher education programs. Though this role has been relatively limited; if we are going to improve student achievement, we must refocus this effort to help states develop the type of personnel that will be needed in the future.

First, it is important to emphasize that in the era of standards-based reform, special education should be specialized. This is necessary if we are to have a professional workforce capable of developing educational programs that minimize the impact of disability while at the same time maximizing opportunities to participate as advocated in chapter 2. There has been a persistent debate in the special education literature over the degree of specialization needed by special educators (Biklen, 1992; Jorgensen, 1997; Milofsky, 1974; Skrtic, 1991; Will, 1986). In 1970, Burton Blatt quoted Alice Metzner's comments on special education, which are still relevant today: "The problem with special education is that it is neither special nor education" (p. 21). This observation reflects the well-documented history of inferior education experienced by many in special education classes at the time (Kirp, 1974).

The notion that once children are placed in special education classes they should receive a different education should be rejected as yet another example of ableism. Though students with disabilities may have individual needs, by and large their education should be based on the same curriculum as that of nondisabled students. This is why advocates worked so hard to amend the IDEA in 1997 and continue to support No Child Left Behind—to specifically require IEP teams to address issues of curricular access. Deafness does not mean students should not be taking physics, and dyslexia should not preclude access to great literature. Viewed in this light, special education should not mean providing a different curriculum but providing the vehicle by which students with disabilities can access the curriculum and the means to address their unique needs. The role of the special educator thus requires a good deal of specialized knowledge and skill.

Unfortunately, one by-product of the desire for greater inclusion, particularly for students with cognitive disabilities, has been minimizing the need for specialization (Biklen, 1992; Jorgensen, 1997; Will, 1986). In many states, specialized preparation of special education personnel is minimal and requires preparation as a general educator first. Though this may be desirable in the ideal, an emphasis on general education may take away from the need to learn specialized skills and also may inadvertently contribute to the increasing shortage of personnel for special education and related services. If we accept that the role of these people is to help disabled children access the curriculum and meet the unique needs that arise out of their disability, the need for specialization should be obvious. Teaching Braille, knowing how to help students use communication devices, developing behavioral interventions for a student with autism, and providing a comprehensive approach to accommodating the curriculum for a dyslexic student are but a few of the specialized competencies required to ensure full access to education for students with disabilities. Though it is important to increase the skills of regular educators in accommodating and modifying instruction for students with disabilities, it is unrealistic to assume that all regular educators can develop these skills. The lack of availability of specialized support has been cited in recent research as a reason some students were placed in segregated settings, although they otherwise may have been served in inclusive settings (Hanson et al., 2001). Well-trained special educators are needed to assist general educators and the students they teach in inclusive settings and at times to provide intensive instruction outside those settings.

The need to ensure that special educators learn specialized skills is not an argument for traditional categorical (by disability) special education teacher-training programs. Such programs often reinforce existing approaches that focus on the characteristics of disability to the exclusion of access to the general curriculum. Further, some traditional programs are not teaching the specialized skills required by IEPs. For instance, when I worked at OSEP, advocates for the blind complained that many "vision teachers" could not teach Braille. A review of existing teacher-training programs for the vision impaired by the U.S. Department of Education revealed that many programs did not teach this skill. This lack of focus on disability-specific skills is not confined to blindness. Examples of such deficiencies exist in virtually all areas of special education teacher preparation. A number of deaf advocates have complained that many teachers of the deaf are not proficient signers, a complaint that reflects the controversies about oralism in the field. Learning disability advocates have been so concerned about both regular and special educational personnel's lack of appropriate skills that the National Center on Learning Disabilities sponsored a summit on teacher preparation in 1996. A major concern emerged over the lack of appropriate training in the area of teaching reading to dyslexic students.

We need to develop clear standards for special education teacher-preparation programs. These standards must recognize disabled students' specific needs and ensure that teachers have the skills necessary to develop appropriate individualized programs. The federal government should take the lead in this effort and support the development of national standards for the preparation of personnel for special education and related services. These programs must explicitly challenge the ableist assumption that the manner in which nondisabled children perform school-related tasks is always the preferred goal for students with disabilities. Teachers must be able to give these students the skills they need to perform at their maximum level and give the students' regular education teachers the help they need to ensure maximum access to the curriculum. Without special education teachers who have disability-specific skills, children with disabilities will continue to lack the skills they need to efficiently and effectively deal with the demands of school and life.

In order to assure that students with disabilities receive appropriate supports and interventions designed to promote better outcomes, general educators also will need improved preparation in the area of disabilities. Again, the federal government should take the lead in promoting improved teacher-preparation programs. Suffice it to say that both the quality and the quantity of special education teachers and general education teachers must increase. The law is meaningless without qualified implementers. A two-pronged federal approach with strong state partnerships is thus necessary to meet this need.

On the supply side, the usual way the IDEA has addressed shortages has been through grants to universities, which provide stipends to a small number of students. This has been inefficient and ineffective. For instance, analysis conducted by the U.S. Department of Education in 2002 concerning shortages of speech therapists showed that 59 percent of special education administrators reported that these shortages hindered their efforts to hire qualified people; 12 percent hired unqualified providers (U.S. Department of Education, 2003). The report went on to warn of future personnel shortages due to the aging of the speech and language pathology workforce; 49 percent of the approximately 49,700 therapists are 45 or older, with a much smaller cohort following.

A more aggressive approach to training qualified special education teachers would be to offer loan forgiveness for students who work a minimum of five years within the field after completing school. This approach has been successful with other programs and would create a powerful incentive to enter the field that could help reduce shortages.

The federal government should also fund research and projects that develop and promulgate state-of-the-art practices in the preparation of both regular and special education personnel to serve students with disabilities. The work of teaching and supporting disabled students is complex; teachers have to know how to bring this diverse group of students to high levels of achievement—it is not enough to simply certify people to teach. Ultimately, the effectiveness of various teacher-preparation programs can be studied. This is a particularly critical issue for special education, where shortages are extreme and the temptation for "quick-fix" programs is great. Adding to this complexity is the diversity of the populations served, from low-birth-weight babies to college-bound high schoolers with dyslexia.

This may be an opportune time to reconceptualize the federal role in assuring an adequate supply of highly qualified personnel, given changes made in IDEA 2004. Most important, the new law conforms with NCLB requirements concerning highly qualified providers and emphasizes the need for special education teachers to demonstrate competence in the core academic areas they are teaching (IDEA 2004, Section 602 [10] A, C, F). This change makes sense in an era of standards-based reform in which students are being tested in core academic subjects and, in many states, experiencing high-stakes consequences. In my view, this change also may promote more inclusive practices, as many special education teachers may be unqualified to teach core academic subjects. Thus, some students who are currently segregated, particularly those who are not part of alternate assessment programs, may be more appropriately placed in mainstream academic classes with accommodations and supports.

Therefore, the need to improve the skills of special education teachers so they can work with their general education counterparts on accommodating instruction for students with disabilities will grow. Furthermore, these teachers will need to become more proficient in providing interventions that address the unique needs that arise out of children's disabilities. As more children move into mainstream general education, teachers need to learn more about how disability impacts curriculum acquisition and how they can accommodate instruction.

Thus, to reach the goal of graduating highly qualified teachers, the teacher-training discretionary program of Part D should focus on state-of-the-art teacher-training programs for both regular education and special education personnel. Grants to higher education should support innovation in both preservice and in-service training. National institutes and research centers should be established to develop and disseminate best practice. These efforts should be closely coordinated with state professional development programs. Therefore, under this proposal, an enhanced federal commitment of loan forgiveness and support should be accompanied by greater accountability at the state level, with states being required to demonstrate that their programs meet statewide and local needs for highly qualified teachers and related services personnel.

In addition to this increased focus on state-level accountability, there is a need to reinforce the enhanced federal role, established in the 1997 reauthorization and continued in IDEA 2004, in the area of teacher preparation for students with low-incidence disabilities, that is, disabilities that occur in less than 1 percent of the population. Most states do not have sufficient demand for such highly specialized staff to justify the establishment of programs. For instance, the need to have teachers who can teach Braille to blind students is very small in relationship to the entire workforce, involving less than one tenth of 1 percent of students. Small states will need only a few new Braille teachers every year. Given the lack of feasibility for each state to have programs in each of these specialties, the federal government should assume increased responsibility in this area. An important step forward would be for the federal government to subsidize the development and maintenance of regionally based programs to serve the needs of these populations.

### 9. Expand parent training centers.

Parent Training Centers have been funded under the IDEA for many years. Though these centers reach a relatively small number of parents due to lack of funding, they are often models of parent empowerment that enable parents to advocate for their children. Centers give parents training that helps them understand the nature of their child's disability as well as the complexity of special education law. Given that students with disabilities whose parents are highly involved in their education experience significantly improved outcomes (Wagner et al., 1993), an important strategy for improving results should be expansion of these centers. Particular emphasis should be on expanding efforts in minority and low-income areas, where parents are least apt to have this training and where the cumulative impact of poverty and disability can have an even greater negative impact on educational outcomes.

### 10. Cautiously implement treatment-resistant models of disability identification.

A major new movement in special education policy concerns the movement toward the identification of treatment-resistant models of disability. Essentially, this policy seeks to require that certain students first be exposed to intensive regular education interventions before they are designated as disabled under the IDEA; that is, they are eligible to receive special education services. This change in the disability identification process holds promise for getting help to children earlier while avoiding inappropriate labeling of children, particularly those with learning disability (LD) or serious emotional disturbance (SED). These approaches also comport well with the concepts of universal design developed in chapter 4. Finally, these models may positively impact the long-standing problem of inappropriate overplacement of minority students in special education (Donavan & Cross, 2002; Losen & Orfield, 2002). However, though this is a promising policy development, there are sound reasons for moving cautiously in this area.

The treatment-resistant approach has been heavily influenced by research in the area of learning disabilities. As discussed in chapter 3, this research has demonstrated that many students who are identified as LD might not have developed reading-related difficulties if they had received appropriate interventions in kindergarten and the primary grades. This assertion is based on years of high-quality research conducted at the National Institutes of Health, which demonstrated that roughly 18 percent of children experience significant early reading difficulty. Further, well-structured early interventions with an emphasis on phonemic awareness were shown to greatly reduce the number of these students who experience persistent reading difficulty. Intervention studies have shown that only a relatively small number of students, 1.4–5.4 percent, depending on the study, do not respond to these interventions. Given this finding, the study's authors rightly condemn current practices associated with LD, specifically, allowing children to struggle with reading in the primary grades before providing interventions. This practice, which is largely driven by the discrepancy definition of LD, virtually guarantees that students will be inappropriately identified as LD and, more important, as time goes by, decreases the likelihood these children will become proficient readers (Lyon et al., 2001).

Lyon and colleagues propose some rather sweeping changes to policy and practice. It is noteworthy that they identify the solution to this problem as largely a regular education issue, with special education playing a supportive role. Given the prevalence of early reading difficulty in young children, they argue that early intensive intervention for students experiencing early reading difficulty should become an integral part of K–3 education. They emphasize that these children are easy to identify and that the longer we wait, the greater the likelihood that they will develop into disabled readers. This is not to say that all children will become facile readers with these interventions. Some children have deep-seated problems with reading and do not respond fully to these interventions, and they will likely need significant support throughout their school careers. However, these students also benefit from these interventions, although not as dramatically. An important point these authors make is that unless we get a handle on the early reading issue, we will not have the resources to support those who truly have LD. As standards-based reform progresses, it is becoming increasingly clear that most students with LD are struggling; many need more, not less, support. This cannot happen if our special education system is overwhelmed with inappropriate referrals.

On the policy level, Lyon and colleagues seek substantive, far-reaching change. They call for the abandonment of the IQ/discrepancy model for determining the existence of LD and seek an identification system that would require the provision of interventions before identification. They argue against the current exclusionary aspect of the federal LD definition, that is, that LD is not the result of other conditions that impede learning such as inadequate instructional opportunities or cultural issues. They argue further that the brain and the environment operate in a reciprocal fashion and that excluding needy children from the specialized services they need is wrong.

The LD definition issues have been with us since the early years of IDEA implementation. However, crafting an alternative system is fraught with difficulty and carries a significant risk of unintended consequences. Advocates fear that changes may result in students with LD being denied services, while educators fear burgeoning inappropriate referrals.

IDEA 2004 does not go as far as these authors advocate, but it does provide important policy changes that support the response to intervention. There are opportunities to implement new approaches without the potential negative implications of mandated wholesale change. First, the new law does not require the use of "severe discrepancy" for learning disability identification purposes and may use response to research-based intervention to determine eligibility; that is, school districts could implement early reading interventions prior to referring children to special education (IDEA 2004, Section 614 [C]). Further, the law allows the use of up to 15 percent of IDEA funds in combination with other funds to provide, among other things, early intervention services for students experiencing reading or behavior difficulties. Thus, children in the early grades could get support without having to be labeled (IDEA 2004, Section 613 [F]). Finally, the law increases the states' responsibility for monitoring and intervening in school districts that have demonstrated an overplacement of minority children in special education (IDEA 2004, Section 616 [A]), which may provide an impetus for some school districts to implement early interventions in regular education for students experiencing reading and behavior problems.

The new law, therefore, provides opportunities to implement treatment-resistant models that may benefit disabled students by providing earlier intervention while at the same time having a positive impact on the overplacement of minority students. (These approaches are concrete examples of universal design, as discussed in chapter 4.) First, the law seeks to insure that general education has provided significant scientifically based interventions before referral is made, thereby decreasing the likelihood that students would be referred because they have not been taught properly. This differs significantly from traditional prereferral approaches that have focused on teacher methodologies and strategies, not on systematic early programmatic interventions, and that often have not occurred until the intermediate grades or later. Prereferral, the first stage of the special education process, has generally been viewed as a method of helping prevent the misidentification of students with disabilities and reduce the number of inappropriate referrals (Fuchs et al., 1990; Garcia & Ortiz, 1988). In contrast, treatment-resistant models imply a functional definition of prereferral that focuses specifically on reading and behavior, two areas identified in the literature as important for helping all children succeed in school. Second, this approach avoids the "wait and fail" model of disability determination, thus decreasing the likelihood that young children will experience devastating failure early in their school career. It is important to note that "treatment resisters" are also helped by these interventions; they simply are not sufficient. Third, this approach explicitly acknowledges that disability determination is influenced by context; that is, the way general education serves students has a major impact on disability identification. The research shows clearly that lack of appropriate instruction can "cause" reading disability. It is important to acknowledge that all students who are significantly behind in reading by fourth grade are functionally disabled, whether due to dyslexia or to poor instruction. The traditional approach of trying to find intrinsic causality for disability as the basis for special education intervention misses the broader issue of the efficacy of the school district's reading approaches for all students.

There are some interesting parallels between the research on behavioral disabilities and that on early reading. Given that behavioral problems are the second major cause of referrals to special education, the relevance to the overplacement of minority students in special education should be clear (Donavan & Cross, 2002). For instance, the likelihood of African American students being placed in programs for students with emotional disturbance is as much as four times the expected incidence of other students (Los Angeles Unified School District placement data provided to the court monitor in the Chanda Smith litigation).

As discussed in chapter 3, research shows that children are often not identified as having SED until the middle to late elementary years (Duncan et al., 1995). Moreover, delays in identification and intervention can exacerbate emotional and/or behavioral problems, whereas effective early behavioral interventions can be instrumental in mitigating subsequent problems and special education placement (Forness et al., 2000). Therefore, school districts need to develop approaches that address children's social and emotional skills and address behavioral problems that develop prior to referral. In particular, the literature documents the effectiveness of comprehensive schoolwide behavior supports (Horner et al., 2000; Lewis et al., 1998; Scott, 2001; Sprague et al., 2001). Again, as with early reading, the approach of general education to the behavioral needs of primary-grade students can have an impact on the special education identification process.

Although this emerging research consensus is promising, and changes in disability identification provide potential opportunities for all students with disabilities, particularly those with LD and SED, the degree of change required is daunting and calls for a degree of caution on the part of educators and advocates. In short, in order to implement this change in disability determination effectively, school districts will have institute practices that are guided by research in a relatively uniform manner. It is only possible to determine if a child is a treatment resister if all students receive relatively standard treatments. The ability to implement these new approaches on a large-scale basis is likely to encounter a number of obstacles. Among these are (1) the historic inability of schools to change their practices quickly; (2) the conflicts that may arise while implementing these practices with other federal, state, and local policies on discipline and English-language acquisition; (3) the historic autonomy teachers have enjoyed concerning classroom practices; and (4) the lack of financial resources, particularly in low-income districts.

The history of attempts to foster large-scale change in education does not support the notion that education can change quickly. The implementation of PL 94-142 is an interesting case. Thirty years after its enactment we still see widely varying implementation patterns. For instance, even though the law seeks to integrate students with disabilities in accordance with its LRE requirements, states and local districts vary enormously in the degree to which children are educated with their nondisabled peers (U.S. Department of Education, 2003). This is not to say that the law has not promoted greater integration; it has, over time (Hehir, 1997). However, the change has been quite slow and variable. The public education enterprise is large, complicated, and relatively slow to change, but school districts and states should move deliberately in this area.

In the area of learning disability identification, research-based early intervention reading programs are becoming more widespread and are receiving considerable support. However, there is a need for significantly greater research to test these approaches (Fuchs et al., 2004). Another complicating factor may be the receptiveness of many general educators to these approaches. There are still many educators fighting the "reading wars," pitting whole-language advocates against those seeking a more systematic approach to phonics instruction. How these wars play out at the local level may still have an impact on the ability of school districts to implement treatment-resistant disability determination models.

The ongoing implementation of NCLB, with its emphasis on testing students who have limited proficiency in English, further complicates this issue. Though the vast majority of educators and parents support the goal of the speedy acquisition of English-language proficiency, the means school districts employ to achieve this goal may be at odds with the research, with some approaches appearing more ideologically driven than research driven. Full English immersion is an example of this. The use of treatment-resistant models with English-language learners in the primary grades may be compromised by simultaneously learning English and learning to read (Snow, 1998). Thus, treatment-resistant models may be difficult to implement for English-language learners.

The second major problem that treatment-resistant models are likely to experience is teacher autonomy. American education has a long tradition of teacher autonomy, with large numbers of teachers working in "egg-crate" schools, that is, teachers working alone in separate rooms with minimal collaboration (O'Day, 2002). As discussed in chapter 4, researchers have begun to identify the negative consequences of the traditional model of teachers working in isolated, autonomous classrooms and the promise of more collaborative approaches. O'Day's research in Chicago found that effective urban schools were more likely to have collaborative cultures, in which teachers work together on improving the education of urban youth. Richard Elmore's research in District 2 of New York City has demonstrated the power of "distributive leadership," in which educators work collaboratively to improve educational results. Given the complex, knowledge-intensive nature of teaching and learning, instructional improvement is more likely to occur when organizations recognize that different kinds and levels of knowledge are necessary for good instruction. Under distributive leadership, the challenge is to harness these varied skills so that they complement each other and, if there is not enough expertise within the organization, to seek help from outside. Elmore (2004) asserts that this complex work is enhanced when the responsibility of leadership is distributed among educators, thus creating a common culture around instructional improvement for all students and a common set of values to determine how to approach the task. Clearly, treatment-resistant models require a movement away from egg-crate schools and toward schools that implement more universally designed collaborative frameworks in which special educators and general educators work closely to ensure that students have received appropriate early intervention (Elmore, 2004). Though researchers are identifying the efficacy of collaborative approaches, there is little evidence that traditional structures are breaking down. When Elmore, a colleague of mine, speaks in my class, he describes the distributive, collaborative cultures he has researched as being rare and deeply countercultural.

An evaluation I recently conducted of a small, diverse school district that is sincerely attempting to address the issues of earlier intervention and the overplacement of African American students found that the district had very inconsistent approaches to early reading instruction and to discipline and behavior. Though most district leaders identified these inconsistencies as contributing to the problem of overplacement and agreed that it should change, they expressed the belief that change would be difficult due to "teacher autonomy." One described how previous attempts to provide some consistency in the math curriculum had required a lengthy process of "consensus building." Though this district has many impressive and well-credentialed teachers, it is a long way from having a collaborative culture. Furthermore, we cannot be sure that children experiencing early reading problems will receive a more intensive, phonemically based reading approach. In this district, the implementation of treatment-resistant models will require a major cultural shift, and there is no reason to believe that it is atypical. The movement to treatment-resistant models of disability determination will require major cultural change in most districts, and this will take time.

The implementation of more effective early intervention approaches for students experiencing reading and behavior difficulties will require significant resources, and many districts with the highest numbers of minority students may have fewer resources to implement these innovations. To reiterate the findings in the *Hancock* study discussed in chapter 5, the urban and low-income school districts, those whose students may need these approaches the most, are apt to have difficulty implementing them. In general, the picture that emerged of low-income communities' ability to implement treatment-resistant models is sobering. The availability of early intervention services in the area of reading and behavior is spotty. Special education evaluation systems are overtaxed and at times lack comprehensiveness. The good news in this study is that the affluent districts appeared to be implementing research-based best practices and that special education was largely effective. In these districts, treatment-resistant models may prove relatively easy to implement. Furthermore, though the low-income districts had difficulty implementing these strategies, district leaders (principals and special education directors) were aware of the research. Funding was the largest impediment to implementing new models. And although the study was limited in scope, it appears that unless the issue of funding is addressed in the low-income districts where many minority students reside, the opportunity to address the overplacement of minority students in special education that is provided by treatment-resistant models of disability identification may be limited. However, given the priority established in IDEA 2004 for states to address the issue of overplacement, states and local school districts could combine funds to demonstrate more effective practices.

## RECOMMENDATIONS REGARDING TREATMENT-RESISTANT MODELS OF DISABILITY IDENTIFICATION

Given the promises of treatment-resistant models in special education identification and the difficulties their implementation will raise, the following recommendations seem appropriate:

1. *Start out with model demonstration programs that are carefully implemented and documented.* This strategy has worked successfully in the past in special education and has resulted in significant large-scale innovation. Early intervention programs, inclusion programs for students with significant cognitive disabilities, transition programs for adolescents, and preschool programs are examples of widely adopted practices that started out as either model demonstration programs or "systems change" grants. Given their national significance, these programs all began with significant federal support under the IDEA Part C (discretionary grant) program. Given the importance of this issue nationally, it is worthy of similar support.

2. *Ensure funding.* The inadequate level of funding for low-income districts, where minorities are more likely to be enrolled, will likely greatly inhibit the implementation of these new identification models. States and the federal government should examine the adequacy of funds to implement these approaches before requiring LEAs to implement them. Local capacity-building grants under the IDEA that enable states to target federal funds for certain districts could be very helpful here. These grants allow states to target IDEA money to certain school districts to promote innovation or program improvement.

3. *Ensure that once students are identified, special education services are powerful and beneficial.* For students who have disabilities who have not benefited sufficiently from general education interventions, special education programs must be based on comprehensive evaluations, with IEPs designed to confer benefit in accordance with the recommendations in chapter 2. This means that students' programs address the needs that arise out of their disabilities while at the same time ensuring access to challenging curriculum. For instance, students with dyslexia will continue to need powerful intervention around their reading (Shaywitz, 2003; Torgesen, 2000; Torgesen et al., 2001) while being provided with access to a curriculum that accommodates their likely problems with reading, writing, and spelling. Though some interventions may require removal from the general education class, unnecessary segregation should be avoided.

4. *Conduct additional research.* Although there is promising research in the area of treatment-resistant models of disability and in the universal design of early reading and behavior intervention and support programs, much more research must be done. For instance, in reading more research is needed that relates to comprehension. Further, there is a need for implementation research to identify how these new approaches can be replicated most efficiently and effectively. The federal government should fund this research under Part D of the IDEA.

The movement toward treatment-resistant models of disability identification is a hopeful development that begins to put the onus of inappropriate placement in special education more in the court of general education. Further, these models also provide students with disabilities who may not yet be identified with services that will lessen the impact of their disability and at the same time promote the concept of universal design. More than ever, special educators must join with general education colleagues to implement the types of programs all children need to succeed. All levels of government, local, state, and federal, should partner to provide the resources necessary to promote this significant and overdue reform. Within this context, universally designed treatment-resistant approaches can add an important element of educational improvement in both disability and racial equity enforcement efforts.

## SUMMARY

Policy drives much of the education of students with disabilities. Therefore, understanding federal and district policies is vitally important. However, policy is constantly evolving and subject to change. Therefore, policy recommendations included in this chapter may or may not at any given time reflect federal or state policy. The proposals outlined above seek to encourage an optimal environment for improving educational results for students with disabilities and in some respects advocate changes in current policy. However, it is important to add a word of caution. The environment of standards-based reform and high-stakes testing is relatively new, and there are many unknowns. Therefore, policy makers and implementers need to be flexible and respond to new situations as they arise. As a wise person once warned me, "Today's policy solution is tomorrow's policy problem."

Further, it is important to note that though policy in special education tends to be federally driven, there has always been more flexibility in special education policy at both the state and local levels than most assume. The tremendous variability in implementation patterns attests to that fact. As a general rule, as long as basic federal requirements are met, states and local school districts are free to innovate. Local districts or states can implement most of the recommendations in this chapter under existing federal law. School officials and parents do not have to wait for Congress to act.

More important to the policies per se are the values that guide them. Being clear about the value of—and the right of all students with disabilities to—a quality education that minimizes the impact of their disability while maximizing their future options will help ensure beneficial future policies. We may come to a day when policies and regulations matter far less than they do today, a day when students with disabilities receive what they need as a matter of course, a day in which ableism is eliminated. I hope this book helps promote that future.

# Epilogue

I would like to conclude this book with an update on Joe Ford. He is currently entering his senior year at Harvard College and is progressing along with his classmates, taking a full load of classes and doing well. He has found most of his professors willing to accommodate his needs. However, access to higher education has not gone as smoothly for Joe as it could have. In a very real sense, Joe's experience at Harvard is a metaphor for the content of this book.

That is, Joe's mere presence at the school represents progress for the school and for society. Had Joe not had the inclusive opportunities that enabled him to access a quality K–12 education, he would never have been able to meet the criteria for admission. As such, he represents a new generation of students who have benefited from Section 504 and the IDEA and are breaking down historic barriers. There were no doubt a number of "Joes" in that institution I visited as an undergraduate, but countless disabled people in the past did not have the benefit of today's more benevolent policy environment.

However, Joe has faced barriers to access that were completely avoidable. For example, he has had great difficulty getting access to digitized text, which is necessary for his screen reader. During his first years at Harvard he often had to wait weeks to get digitized copies of readings, which made it difficult for him to keep up in certain classes. (He enlisted family members as readers to close this gap.) However, during his junior year, Joe began to notice improvements in the delivery of his reformatted books. By the end of his junior year, entire books were being delivered in a day or two—a far cry from the 50 pages a day Harvard had delivered the previous year.

Library access, too, has been particularly difficult for Joe. For instance, during his freshman year, if he wanted access to a journal article for research he was doing, he was told to obtain a Xerox copy and take it to a special technology center to be scanned and later sent to him in a digitized format via email. This process often took two weeks. How could anyone do research that way? There is a simple solution incorporating the principles of universal design that could enable his full and reasonable access to the library. The Harvard library system is one of the largest in the world and has high-speed scanners throughout. Joe has suggested that the library allow him to drop off the material he needs scanned at one of these scanners to be entered by a "work study" student, of which there are many throughout the library, to perform this task on the spot. Though he is getting readings quicker, so far the university has been unwilling to do this procedure which would give him immediate access.

Another battleground has been the university shuttle service, which only recently added a limited number of vehicles with wheelchair lifts. However, the lifts frequently break down, resulting in last-minute emergency calls for the segregated "special" vans disabled students used before Joe's junior year. So Joe must plan each day ahead of time, making certain that the regular shuttle from his house, which is about three-quarters of a mile from the campus, has a working lift or ordering a special van as needed. The lack of reliable scheduled shuttles creates a number of access issues for him, particularly in winter when the sidewalks of Cambridge are barely accessible for anyone. Had the transportation been universally designed from the beginning by purchasing a fleet of accessible shuttles with dependable lifts, Joe would have equal access. This also might ultimately be cheaper for the university, as it would eliminate the cost of special trips and the labor they entail. (It is true that students with disabilities sometimes need special vans due to inclement weather or other circumstances that make door-to-door service necessary.)  Joe is not the only student, or faculty member for that matter, who needs accessible transportation.

As far as campus life is concerned, Joe has experienced some degree of ableism. For instance, during his freshman year, a fellow student posted a sign on her door, "Harvard Rules, Yale Drools." Joe, who does drool, took offense and sought to have the sign removed. The dorm proctor and Joe's freshman dean refused, citing "free speech" concerns. Would the reaction have been the same had the sign contained a racial epithet or homophobic taunt? Furthermore, had the proctor handled this incident differently, he could have provided an opportunity for nondisabled students to address what appeared to be unintended ableist attitudes. One of the greatest advantages of having a diverse student body is the learning opportunities it provides for all students. Given the leadership role many of these Harvard students will likely play in the world, it is a shame that this opportunity was missed.

As is the case with most educational institutions, Harvard would benefit greatly by confronting ableism. When Joe was applying, an admissions officer told him and his mother that the school does not do much "hand holding" for its disabled students. Joe has never sought that. All he and most disabled students want and need is access, and it is clear that the university has yet to develop policies and practices that fully enable that to occur. Furthermore, most issues encountered by Joe and other disabled students I know could be addressed through universal design.

Overall, however, Joe is positive about his experience at Harvard. He believes he is getting a high-quality education that will prepare him well for graduate study. He spent last summer in Ecuador studying the literature of that country and doing an internship at a nonprofit that serves disabled children and adults. He is planning to do his senior thesis on the behavior and impact of small states during the Cuban Missile Crisis, after which he plans to pursue an advanced degree in political science. Joe is also finding "his voice" as a budding disability activist. Recently he wrote an op-ed piece for the *Harvard Crimson* concerning the Terry Schiavo case and its implications for withholding medical treatment from disabled people. His remarks were picked up by the *Wall Street Journal*. I have no doubt that Joe is going to have an illustrious career.

I am also optimistic that a new generation of disabled students like Joe, and their allies, will continue on the path of progress that began with access to education in the mid-seventies and will reach its goal when disabled people attain true equality. Improving educational opportunity will continue to play a central role in that movement. I hope this book will, in a small way, help reach that day.

# References

Allington, R. L., & McGill-Franzen, A. (1989). School response to reading failure: Instruction for chapter one and special education students grade two, four, and eight. *Elementary School Journal, 89,* 529–542.

American Speech-Language Hearing Association. (2002). *A workload analysis approach for establishing speech-language caseload standards in the schools: Guidelines.* Retrieved June 2005 from http://professional.asha.org/resources/.

Parrish, T. (2002). Racial disparities in identification, funding, and provision of special education. In D. J. Losen & G. Orfield (Eds.), *Racial inequity in special education* (pp. 15–38). Cambridge, MA: Harvard Education Press.

Artiles, A., Rueda, R., Salazar, J. J., & Higareda, I. (2002). English-language learner representation in special education in California urban school districts. In D. J. Losen & G. Orfield (Eds.), *Racial inequity in special education* (pp. 117-136). Cambridge, MA: Harvard Education Press.

Baynton, D. C. (1996). *Forbidden signs: American culture and the campaign against sign language.* Chicago: University of Chicago Press.

Bérubé, M. (1996). *Life as we know it: A father, a family, and an exceptional child.* New York: Pantheon Books.

Biklen, D. (1992). *Schooling without labels: Parents, educators, and inclusive education.* Philadelphia: Temple University Press.

Blatt, B. (1970). *Exodus from pandemonium.* Boston: Allyn & Bacon.

Brown, L., Schwarz, P., Udvari-Solner, A., Kampschroer, E. F., Johnson, F., Jorgenson, J., & Gruenewald, L. (1991). How much time should students with severe intellectual disabilities spend in regular education classrooms and elsewhere? In J. Rogers (Ed.), *Inclusion: Moving beyond our fears* (pp. 111–122). Bloomington, IN: Phi Delta Kappa Center for Evaluation, Development, and Research.

Coleman, M. R. (2000). *Conditions for special education teaching: CEC Commission technical report.* Arlington, VA: Council for Exceptional Children.

Count me in: Special education in an era of reform. (2004, January). *Education Week* [Special issue].

Courtin, C. (2000). The impact of sign language on the cognitive development of deaf children: The case of theories of the mind. *Journal of Deaf Studies and Deaf Education, 5,* 266–276.

D'Antonio, M. (2004). *The state boys rebellion.* New York: Simon & Schuster.

Donavan, S. M., & Cross, C. T. (Eds.). (2002). *Minority students in special and gifted education.* Washington, DC: National Academy Press.

Duncan, B., Forness, S. R., & Hartsough, C. (1995). Students identified as seriously emotionally disturbed in day treatment: Cognitive, psychiatric, and special education characteristics. *Behavioral Disorders, 20,* 238-252.

Eber, L., & Keenan, S. (2004). Collaboration with other agencies: Wraparound and systems of care for children and youths with emotional and behavioral disorders. In R. B. Rutherford, M. M. Quinn, & S. R. Mathur (Eds.), *Handbook of research in emotional and behavioral disorders.* New York: Guilford Press.

Elmore, R. F. (2004). *School reform from the inside out: Policy, practice, and performance.* Cambridge, MA: Harvard Education Press.

Ferguson, P. M., & Asch, A. (1989). Lessons from life: Personal and parental perspectives on school, childhood and disability. In D. Biklen, D. Ferguson, & A. Ford (Eds.), *Schooling and disability: Eighty-eighth yearbook of the National Society for the Study of Education: Part II* (pp. 108–141). Chicago: University of Chicago Press.

Ford, P. (1993). *Something to be gained: A family's long road to inclusive schooling.* In J. Rogers (Ed.), *Inclusion: Moving beyond our fears* (pp. 101–111). Bloomington, IN: Phi Delta Kappa Center for Evaluation, Development, and Research.

Forness, S. R., Serna, L. A., Nielson, E., Lambros, K., Hale, M. J., & Kavale, K. A. (2000). A model for early detection and primary prevention of emotional or behavioral disorders. *Education and Treatment of Children, 23,* 325–346.

Fuchs, D., & Fuchs, L. S. (1994). Inclusive schools movement and the radicalization of special education reform. *Exceptional Children, 60,* 294–309.

Fuchs, D., & Fuchs, L. S. (1995). What's "special" about special education? *Phi Delta Kappan, 76,* 522–530.

Fuchs, D., Fuchs, L., Bahr, M. W., Fernstrom, P., & Stecker, P. J. (1990). Pre-referral intervention: A prescriptive approach. *Exceptional Children, 56,* 493–513.

Fuchs, D., Fuchs, L., & Comptom, D. (2004). Identifying reading disabilities by response-to-instruction: Specifying measures and criteria. *Learning Disabilities Quarterly, 27,* 216–227.

Fuchs, L. S., & Fuchs, D. (1999). *Accountability and assessment in the 21st century for students with learning disabilities.* Nashville, TN: Peabody College of Vanderbilt University.

Garcia, S. B., & Ortiz, A. A. (1988, June). Preventing inappropriate referral of language minority students to special education. *National Clearinghouse for Bilingual Education: New Focus, 5,* 1–12.

Gartner, A., & Lipsky, D. K. (1996). Inclusion, school restructuring, and the remaking of American society. *Harvard Educational Review, 66,* 762–796.

Giangreco, M., Edelman, S., Luiselli, T., & Macfarland, S. (1997). Helping or hovering? The effects of instructional assistant proximity on students with disabilities. *Exceptional Children, 64,* 7–18.

Groce, N. E. (1985). *Everyone here spoke sign language: Hereditary deafness on Martha's Vineyard.* Cambridge, MA: Harvard University Press.

Gruner, A. (2004). *Defining inclusion: Working toward a shared language among policymakers, researchers, and practitioners.* Unpublished manuscript.

Hanson, M. J., Horn, E., Sandall, S., Beckman, P., Morgan, M., Marquart, J., Barnwell, D., & Chou, H. (2001). After preschool inclusion: Children's educational pathways over the early school years. *Exceptional Children, 68*(1), 65–83.

Harry, B., Klingner, J. K., Sturgess, K. M., & Moore, R. (2002). Of rocks and soft places: Using qualitative methods to investigate the processes that result in disproportionality. In D. J. Losen & G. Orfield (Eds.), *Racial inequity in special education* (pp. 71–92). Cambridge, MA: Harvard Education Press.

Hehir, T. (1990). Chapter 9: Conclusions. In *The impact of due process on the programmatic decisions of special education directors.* Unpublished doctoral dissertation, Harvard Graduate School of Education, Cambridge, MA.

Hehir, T. (1997). IDEA has led to improved results for students with disabilities: A response to Lipsky and Gartner. *Harvard Educational Review, 67,* 596–601.

Hehir, T. (2002). IDEA and disproportionality: Federal enforcement, effective advocacy, and strategies for change. In D. J. Losen & G. Orfield

(Eds.), *Racial inequity in special education* (pp. 219–238). Cambridge, MA: Harvard Education Press.

Hehir, T., & Gamm, S. (1999). Special education: From legalism to collaboration. In J. Heubert (Ed.), *Law and school reform* (pp. 205–227). New Haven, CT: Yale University Press.

Hehir, T., Gruner, A., Karger, J., & Katzman, L. (2003, June). Hancock v. Driscoll: *Special education assessment.* Unpublished report.

Hehir, T., Gruner, A., Karger, J., & Katzman, L. (2004, August). *Brookline High School Tutorial Program: Year 2 evaluation.* Unpublished report.

Heubert, J. P., & Hauser, R. M. (Eds.). (1999). *High stakes: Testing for tracking, promotion and graduation.* Washington, DC: National Academy Press.

Hocutt, A. M. (1996). Effectiveness of special education: Is placement the critical factor? *Future of Children, 6*(1), 77–102.

Horner, R. H., Sugai, G., & Horner, H. F. (2000). A schoolwide approach to student discipline. *School Administrator,* (February), 20–24.

Individuals with Disabilities Education Act Amendments of 1997, Pub. L. No. 105-17, §1400, 37 Stat. 111 (1997).

Jacobs, L. (1989). *A deaf adult speaks out.* Washington, DC: Gallaudet University Press.

Johnson, L. (1996). The Braille literacy crisis for children. *Journal of Visual Impairment and Blindness, 90,* 276–278.

Jorgensen, C. (1997). *Restructuring high schools for all students: Taking inclusion to the next level.* Baltimore: Paul Brooks.

Karger, J. (2002). *Access to the general curriculum: Meaning and implementation.* Unpublished manuscript.

Katzman, L. I. (2001). *The effects of high-stakes testing on students with disabilities: What do we know?* Unpublished qualifying paper, Harvard Graduate School of Education, Cambridge, MA.

Katzman, L. I. (2004). *Students with disabilities and high-stakes testing: What can the students tell us?* Unpublished doctoral dissertation, Harvard Graduate School of Education, Cambridge, MA.

Kauffman, J. M., & Hallahan, D. P. (Eds.). (1995). *The illusion of full inclusion: A comprehensive critique of a current special education bandwagon.* Austin, TX: Pro-Ed.

Kirp, D. L. (1974). The great sorting machine: Special education trends and issues. *Phi Delta Kappan, 55,* 521–525.

Kliewer, C., Fitzgerald, L. M., Meyer-Mork, J., Hartman, P., English-Sand, P., & Raschke, D. (2004). Citizenship for all in the literate community: An ethnography of young children with significant disabilities in inclusive early childhood settings. *Harvard Educational Review, 74,* 373–403.

Koretz, D. M., & Hamilton, L. S. (2000). Assessment of students with disabilities in Kentucky: Inclusion, student performance, and validity. *Education Evaluation and Policy Analysis, 22,* 255–272.

Lane, H. (1995). The education of deaf children: Drowning in the mainstream and the sidestream. In J. M. Kauffman & D. P. Hallahan (Eds.), *The illusion of full inclusion: A comprehensive critique of a current special education bandwagon* (pp. 275–287). Austin, TX: Pro-Ed.

Lewis, T., & Sugai, G. (1999). Effective behavior support: A systems approach to proactive schoolwide management. *Focus on Exceptional Children, 31*(6).

Lewis, T., Sugai, G., & Colvin, G. (1998). Reducing problem behavior through a school-wide system of effective behavioral support: Investigation of a school-wide social skills training program and contextual interventions. *School Psychology Review, 27,* 446–460.

Losen, D. J., & Orfield, G. (Eds.). (2002). *Racial inequity in special education.* Cambridge, MA: Harvard Education Press.

Lyon, G. R., Fletcher, J. M., Shaywitz, S. E., Shaywitz, B. A., Torgenson, J. K., Wood, F. B., Shulte, A., & Olson, R. (2001). Rethinking learning disabilities. In C. E. Finn, A. J. Rotherman, & C. R. Hokanson (Eds.), *Rethinking special education for a new century* (pp. 259–287). Washington, DC: Thomas B. Fordham Foundation and Progressive Policy Institute.

Mank, D. M. (2001). *Employability of individuals with mental retardation.* Unpublished paper written for the National Research Council, the Committee on Disability Determination for Mental Retardation, Department of Curriculum and Instruction, Indiana University.

Massachusetts Department of Education. (2005). Raw data. Retrieved June 2005 from http://www.doe.mass.edu/assess/

McDonnell, L. M., McLaughlin, M. J., & Morison, P. (1997). *Educating one and all: Students with disabilities and standards-based reform.* Washington, DC: National Academy Press.

McDuffy v. Secretary of Executive Office of Education, 615 N.E.2d 516, 552 (Mass. 1993).

Milofsky, C. D. (1974). Why special education isn't special. *Harvard Educational Review, 44,* 437–458.

Minow, M. (1991). *Making all the difference: Inclusion, exclusion, and American law.* Ithaca, NY: Cornell University Press.

Mutch-Jones, K. (2004). *Collaborative insights: The work of general and special educator pairs in inclusive mathematics classrooms.* Unpublished doctoral dissertation, Harvard University, Cambridge, MA.

National Association of State Boards of Education. (2004). *Policy Update,* 2(12).

National Council on Disability. (1996). *Achieving independence: The challenge for the 21st century. A decade of progress in disability policy setting for the future.* Washington, DC: Author.

National Council on Disability. (2001). *Back to school on civil rights.* Washington, DC: Independence.

National Federation of the Blind. (n.d.). *What is Braille and what does it mean to the blind?* [Online]. Available at http://www.nfb.org/books/books1/ifblnd03.htm

New York State Department of Education. (2001). *Reforming education for students with disabilities.* Albany: New York State Education Department, Office of Vocational and Educational Services for Individuals with Disabilities.

Nolet, V., & McLaughlin, M. J. (2000). *Accessing the general curriculum: Including students with disabilities in standards-based reform.* Thousand Oaks, CA: Corwin Press.

Oberti v. Board of Education, 995 F.2d 1204 (3rd Cir. 1993).

O'Day, J. (2002). Complexity, accountability, and school improvement. *Harvard Educational Review, 72,* 293–329.

Overboe, J. (1999). "Difference in itself": Validating disabled people's lived experience. *Body and Society, 5*(4), 17–29.

Pittman, P., & Huefner, D. S. (2001). Will the courts go bi-bi? IDEA 1997, the courts and deaf education. *Exceptional Children, 67,* 187–198.

Postsecondary Education Programs. (2005). Website for the deaf. Retrieved September 2005 from http://www.pepnet.org

President's Commission on Excellence in Special Education. (2002). *A new era: Revitalizing special education for children and families.* Washington, DC: U.S. Department of Education.

Prinz, P. M., & Strong, M. (1998). ASL proficiency and English literacy within a bilingual deaf education model of instruction. *Topics in Language Disorders, 18*(4), 47–60.

Rauscher, L., & McClintock, J. (1996). Ableism and curriculum design. In M. Adams, L. A. Bell, & P. Griffen (Eds.), *Teaching for diversity and social justice* (pp. 198–231). New York: Routledge.

Reagan, T. (1985). The deaf as a linguistic minority: Educational consider-ations. *Harvard Educational Review, 55,* 265–277.

Rehabilitation Act of 1973, 29 U.S.C. 504, § 794.

Reville, S. T. (2004). High standards + high stakes = high achievement in Massachusetts. *Phi Delta Kappan, 85,* 591–598.

Rose, D. H., & Meyer, A. (2002). *Teaching every student in the digital age: Universal design for learning.* Alexandria, VA: Association for Supervision and Curriculum Development.

Rousso, H. (1984). Fostering healthy self esteem: Part one. *Exceptional Parent, 14*(8), 9–14.

Rowley v. Board of Education of the Gloversville Enlarged City School, 192 A.D.2d 814, 596 N.Y.S.2d 561 (N.Y. App. Div. 1993).

Sabel, C. F., & Simon, W. H. (2004). Destabilization rights: How public law litigation succeeds. *Harvard Law Review, 117,* 1016–1101.

Sands, D. J., Kozleski, E. B., & French, N. (2000). *Inclusive education for the 21st century: A new introduction to special education.* Belmont, CA: Wadsworth.

Scheerenberger, R. C. (1990). *Public residential services for the mentally retarded. FY 1988–89.* Fairfax, VA: National Association of Superintendents of Public Residential Facilities for the Mentally Retarded.

Schemo, D. J. (2004, August 18). Effort by Bush on education hits obstacles. *New York Times,* p. A1.

Schworm, P. (2004a, September 15). Some top schools on federal watch list. *Boston Globe,* p. B1.

Schworm, P. (2004b, October 3). Federal list spurs soul-searching at affluent schools. *Boston Globe,* p. A1.

Scott, T. M. (2001). A school-wide example of positive behavioral support. *Journal of Positive Behavior Interventions, 3,* 88-94.

Shapiro, J. P. (1994). *No pity: People with disabilities forging a new civil rights movement.* New York: Random House.

Shaywitz, S. (2003). *Overcoming dyslexia: A new and complete science-based program for reading problems at any level.* New York: Alfred A. Knopf.

Sisco, F. H., & Anderson, R. J. (1980). Deaf children's performance of the WISC-R relative to hearing status of parents and child-rearing experiences. *American Annals of the Deaf, 125,* 923–930.

Skrtic, T. M. (1991). The special education paradox: Equity as the way to excellence. *Harvard Educational Review, 61,* 148–206.

Smith, G. (2001, July 20). Backtalk: The brother in the wheelchair. *Essence*, p. 162.

Smith v. Los Angeles Unified School District, United States District Court, No. 93-7044-RSWL.

Snow, C. (Ed.). (1998). *Preventing reading difficulties in young children.* Washington, DC: National Research Council.

Sprague, J., Walker, H., Golly, A., White, K., Myers, D. R., & Shannon, T. (2001). Translating research into effective practice: The effects of a universal staff and student intervention on indicators of discipline and school safety. *Education and Treatment of Children, 24,* 495–511.

Stone, D. A. (1984). *The disabled state.* Philadelphia: Temple University Press.

Stuckless, R. E., & Birch, J. W. (1966). The influence of early manual communication on the linguistic development of deaf children. *American Annals of the Deaf, 111*(2/3), 71–79.

Sugai, G. G., & Horner, R. (2002). The evolution of discipline practices: School-wide positive behavior supports. In J. Luirelli & C. Diament (Eds.), *Behavior psychology in the schools* (vol. 24, pp. 23–50). Binghamton, NY: Haworth Press.

Sugai, G., Sprague, J. R., Horner, R. H., & Walker, H. M. (2000). Preventing school violence: The use of office discipline referrals to assess and monitor school-wide discipline interventions. *Journal of Emotional and Behavioral Disorder, 8,* 94–101.

Thurlow, M. L. (2000). Standards-based reform and students with disabilities: Reflections on a decade of change. *Focus on Exceptional Children, 33*(3), 1–16.

Torgesen, J. K. (2000). Individual differences in response to early intervention in reading: The lingering problem of treatment resisters. *Learning Disabilities Research and Practice, 15*(1), 55–64.

Torgesen, J. K., Alexander, A. W., Wagner, R. K., Rashotte, C. A., Voeller, K. S., & Conway, T. (2001). Intensive remedial instruction for children with severe reading disabilities: Immediate and long-term outcomes from two instructional approaches. *Journal of Learning Disabilities, 34,* 33-58, 78.

Trent, S. (2004). Untitled report prepared for the Independent Monitor, California Unified School District.

U.S. Department of Education. (1995). *Individuals with Disabilities Education Act Amendments of 1995: Reauthorization of the Individuals with Disabilities Education Act.* Washington, DC: Author.

U.S. Department of Education. (1996). *To assure the free and appropriate public education of all children with disabilities* (Eighteenth annual report to Congress on implementation of the Individuals with Disabilities Education Act). Washington, DC: Author.

U.S. Department of Education. (2000). *To assure the free and appropriate public education of all children with disabilities* (Twenty-second annual report to Congress on implementation of the Individuals with Disabilities Education Act). Washington, DC: Author.

U.S. Department of Education. (2003). *To assure the free and appropriate public education of all children with disabilities* (Twenty-fourth annual report to Congress on implementation of the Individuals with Disabilities Education Act). Washington, DC: Author.

Vaughn, G., et al. v. Mayor and City Council of Baltimore, et al. Consent Order, 2000.

Vaughn, S., & Fuchs, L. (2003). Redefining learning disabilities as inadequate response to instruction: The promise and potential problems. *Learning Disabilities Research and Practice, 18,* 137–146.

Vaughn, S., Gersten, R., & Chard, D. J. (2000). The underlying message in LD intervention research: Findings from research syntheses. *Exceptional Children, 67,* 99–114.

Wagner, M., Blackorby, J., Cameto, R., & Newman, L. (1993). *What makes a difference? Influences of postschool outcomes of youth with disabilities* (Report from the National Longitudinal Transition Study of Special Education Students). Washington, DC: U.S. Department of Education.

Wagner, M., & Cameto, R. (2004). *NLTS2 Brief, 3*(2) [Online]. Available at www.ncset.org/publications/default.asp#nlts2

Wagner, M., Newman, L., D'Amico, R., Jay, E. D., Butler-Nalin, P., Marder, C., & Cox, R. (1991). *Youth with disabilities: How are they doing?* Menlo Park, CA: SRI International.

Walker, H. M., Kavanagh, K., Golly, A., Stiller, B., Severson, H. H., & Feil, E. G. (1995). *First steps: Intervention strategies for the early remediation of kindergarten behavior problems.* Eugene: University of Oregon, College of Education, Institute on Violence and Destructive Behavior.

Ward, M. (1988). The many facets of self-determination. *Transition Issues, 5,* 2–3.

Weeber, J. E. (1999). What could I know of racism? *Journal of Counseling and Development, 77*(1), 20–23.

Will, M. (1986). Educating children with learning problems: A shared responsibility. *Exceptional Children, 52,* 411–415.

Wright, B. (1983). *Physical disability: A psycho-social approach.* New York: Harper & Row.

Ysseldyke, J., Dennison, A., & Nelson, R. (2004). *Large-scale assessment and accountability systems: Positive consequences for students with disabilities* (Synthesis Report 51). Minneapolis: University of Minnesota, National Center on Educational Outcomes.

Zwiebel, A. (1987). More on the effects of early manual communication on the cognitive development of deaf children. *American Annals of the Deaf, 132,* 16–20.

# About the Author

Tom Hehir served as director of the U.S. Department of Education's Office of Special Education Programs from 1993 to 1999. As director, he was responsible for federal leadership in implementing the Individuals with Disabilities Education Act (IDEA). Hehir played a leading role in developing the Clinton administration's proposal for the 1997 reauthorization of the IDEA, 90 percent of which was adopted by Congress.

In 1990, Hehir was associate superintendent for the Chicago Public Schools, where he was responsible for special education services and student support services. In this role, he implemented major changes in the special education service delivery system, which enabled Chicago to reach significantly higher levels of compliance with the IDEA and resulted in the eventual removal of the U.S. Department of Education's Office for Civil Rights as overseer.

Hehir served in a variety of positions in the Boston Public Schools from 1978 to 1987, including director of special education from 1983 to 1987. An advocate for children with disabilities in the education system, he has written on special education, special education in the reform movement, due process, and least restrictive environment issues. He is a distinguished scholar at the Educational Development Center in Newton, Massachusetts, where he is a senior policy adviser for the Urban Special Education Leadership Collaborative. Hehir is also the director of the School Leadership Program at the Harvard Graduate School of Education.

# Index